Serving from the Heart

Finding Your Gifts and Talents for Service

UPDATED EDITION

Carol Cartmill & Yvonne Gentile

ABINGDON PRESS
Nashville, Tennessee

SERVING FROM THE HEART

FINDING YOUR GIFTS AND TALENTS FOR SERVICE

Copyright © 2011 by Abingdon Press

ISBN 978-1-426-73599-8

11 12 13 14 15 16 17 18 19 20--10 9 8 7 6 5 4 3 2 1

MANUFACTURED IN THE UNITED STATES OF AMERICA

TABLE OF CONTENTS

FOREWORD

I have an old toolbox that belonged to my great grandfather, Joseph Lorson. He was a carpenter who built homes in Kansas City in the early 1900s. Inside are a myriad of antique tools. Some of the tools I recognize. Others are more mysterious to me; I am not sure how they were used or what purpose they served.

As I look through his box, I am surprised by what seems to be a duplication of tools. There are a half dozen saws—each having a different size or cutting blade. There are different kinds and shapes of chisels and planes. I would love to know when my great grandfather used a particular tool as opposed to another one.

I have debated about what to do with these tools. My father passed them on to me as a gift—a legacy. Should I mount them on a special wall as a tribute to my family heritage? Perhaps I should carefully preserve them in their box and pass them on to my children. Because I am uncertain about what to do with them, they sit in their wooden toolbox in one corner of my garage.

But every once in awhile I have a need for one of these tools—usually a saw, but sometimes a chisel or a hammer. So I take one of the tools from the box and put it to use. Instantly there is a sense of satisfaction as the tool does exactly what it was made to do. These tools were meant to be used! They were designed to build things!

I also have come to appreciate the nuances between some of the tools. The small, thin blade of the trim saw was perfect when I needed to replace a piece of molding in my study. But the large handsaw did the trick when branches were broken and hanging from my trees after an ice storm.

Of course, the metaphors are apparent. Each of us has been given gifts by the Holy Spirit—spiritual tools. Some of the gifts are mysterious; we are not sure how they work or what purpose they serve. Others are readily identified and easy to use. But all are meant to be used—not safely hidden away.

What is more, when we understand which spiritual gifts may be needed for a particular kind of task in the church, help persons identify their spiritual gifts, and then align the right people for the right tasks, the work of the ministry is more effective and the experience of those doing the ministry is full of joy—for they have found the very thing they were gifted to do. It is amazing the difference the right tool can make when approaching a difficult task.

Carol Cartmill and Yvonne Gentile have done a remarkable job of helping hundreds of people discover their spiritual gifts and to begin using them within the church. As a result of their efforts, the people of our church are more effectively serving God, the ministry is growing and expanding, and our members are discovering joy, not drudgery, in their ministry for Christ.

This program is an excellent guide to discovering and making the most of the tools that the Holy Spirit places in our toolboxes.

Adam Hamilton
Senior Pastor
The United Methodist Church of the Resurrection

BEFORE YOU BEGIN

You're about to embark on a journey.

You may be wondering, "Why am I here? Where is this going to lead?" The fact that you've made it to this point is evidence that the Holy Spirit is already at work in your life. This workbook will serve as your guide as you seek to discover certain truths:

> You are uniquely created by God.
> God has given you significant gifts.
> God has a plan and purpose for your life.
> As a Christian, you have been called to serve.

To take it a step further, you will examine how this knowledge impacts the church as a whole. God also has a specific design and purpose for the church—the body of Christ.

> *"For I know the plans I have for you," declares the LORD,*
> *"plans . . . to give you hope and a future." —Jeremiah 29:11*

The Great Invitation

This workbook deals with the workings of the Holy Spirit in the lives of individual Christians and so it is written with the assumption that those who work through it have already accepted Jesus Christ as their Lord and Savior. Perhaps we're being presumptuous. If you have not yet received Christ as your personal savior, let this be an invitation to you: God has plans for you, too. Christ stands at the door knocking, and all you need to do is open up and receive.

Read the following Scriptures, and discover what God has to say to you:

> **John 3:16-17**
> **Romans 5:9-11**
> **Revelation 3:20**

If you have questions, or need someone with whom to talk or pray, speak to your instructor after class. The Christian life is a life of joy, and hope, and an eternal future.

Let's begin our trek. . .

The book you are holding in your hand emerged out of the collective experience of the Spiritual Gifts Discovery Team at The United Methodist Church of the Resurrection in Leawood, Kansas. The Spiritual Gifts Discovery Team is a group of men and women dedicated to helping others discover how God has designed them with the gifts that make it possible for them to be in service within the body of Christ. As we have taught Spiritual Gifts Discovery over the years, we have heard many stories of how people in our church and others have struggled with the concept of serving God. We have heard persons say:

- I'm not qualified to serve God.
- I couldn't possibly have an impact.
- Serving God is a duty; it's not something that should be enjoyed. After all, didn't Christ say, "deny yourself, take up your cross and follow me"?
- There are so many people; I'm not going to be missed.
- That's the pastor's job!
- I've had a bad experience in the past, and I am not going to do that again!

We grieve when we hear statements like this, because we do not believe that this is the way God wants us to think or feel. God's plan for the church calls for each of us to serve in a way that allows us to be effective and to feel personally fulfilled. God purposely created each of us to be unique—with different spiritual gifts, talents, resources, individuality, dreams, and experiences—so that together, as the unified body of Christ, we could accomplish God's work in this world. That may sound overwhelming to some of us. If you're feeling intimidated by that notion, imagine how the disciples must have felt when Jesus commanded them to "go. . . and make disciples of all nations."

The Great Commission

Then Jesus came to them and said, "All authority in heaven and on earth has been given to me. Therefore go and make disciples of all nations, baptizing them in the name of the Father and of the Son and of the Holy Spirit, and teaching them to obey everything I have commanded you. And surely I am with you always, to the very end of the age." —Matthew 28:18-20

The disciples were a rather rag-tag bunch of fellows—mostly uneducated, and certainly not the most reliable or confident group. Just a few weeks earlier they had run for their lives when Jesus was arrested! They had to have been full of self-doubt and overwhelmed about what he was commanding them to do. They had forgotten, or simply did not understand, that Jesus had promised to send them a counselor, comforter, teacher, and helper—the Holy Spirit (see Acts 1:4-5).

The Holy Spirit did arrive as promised (at Pentecost—see Acts 2:1-20). The Holy

Spirit empowered and equipped the disciples to build the church. This was by intentional design. It was God's plan for starting the early church. It is still God's plan for the way the church should function today. The Bible is our primary guidebook for helping us discover God's will for our individual lives and as members of the body of Christ.

At the Church of the Resurrection, we look at the greatest adventure we will ever experience—the life of a disciple—as a journey.

The Journey

Our faith journey begins just like any other journey—from right where we are. For most of us, the first step is to simply begin to explore what it means to be a Christian. We commit to attending worship regularly, support our local church financially, and perhaps attend a Bible study. After a time, we want to go a little deeper, to learn more about the Bible, to get involved in serving regularly. *Serving from the Heart* is designed to help you discover how and where you can best serve—a place and role in which you will both be effective and find fulfillment. To help you accomplish this, we use an acronym called S.T.R.I.D.E.

S.T.R.I.D.E.

No two persons are exactly alike. We have different abilities, dreams, and preferences, among other things. S.T.R.I.D.E.

is an acronym we use to describe the way individual Christians are unique as we take our personal faith journey. Just as we each choose different paths, we also have unique strides as we make our journey. One person walks slowly, the next walks quickly, and another skips all the way! As Christians, we are expected to use our spiritual gifts to serve others and to glorify God. God has created each of us with a specific purpose in mind, giving us varied Spiritual

S.piritual gifts
T.alents
R.esources
I.ndividuality
D.reams
E.xperiences

Gifts, Talents, Resources, Individuality, and Dreams, and incorporating our Experiences in ways that are designed to help us fulfill the Great Commission (Matthew 28:19-20) and live the Greatest Commandment (Matthew 22:37-39). In this book, we will examine these six elements of our unique God-design, and seek to understand God's plan for the church as well as God's purpose for our lives.

Now that we've discussed the "what" and the "why" of our journey, it's time to head down the path. Our first, and foundational, step will be to explore the subject of spiritual gifts, the "S" of our S.T.R.I.D.E. And, speaking of foundations, the primary authority for spiritual gifts is God's Word—the Bible.

Bible

CHAPTER 1

Introduction and Biblical Foundation

Now about the gifts of the Spirit, brothers and sisters,
I do not want you to be uninformed.
—1 Corinthians 12:1

In the Bible passage above, Paul clearly states the importance of the subject of spiritual gifts to Christians. Spiritual gifts and gifts-based ministry are the foundations for understanding how the church is meant to operate, and for understanding our individual roles within the church. In order to understand spiritual gifts, we must examine the context in which they were first given, which begins with Christ's promise to send the Holy Spirit.

As Jesus' earthly ministry was coming to an end, he began to prepare his disciples for the time when they would be called upon to carry on the work he had started. Jesus was returning to God, but he promised the disciples they would not be left alone. The Holy Spirit would come and would teach the disciples all they would need to know in order to continue his ministry.

"Very truly I tell you, all who have faith in me will do the works I have been doing, and they will do even greater things than these, because I am going to the Father. And I will do whatever you ask in my name, so that the Father may be glorified in the Son. You may ask me for anything in my name, and I will do it. If you love me, keep my commands. And I will ask the Father, and he will give you another advocate to help you and be with you forever—the Spirit of truth. The world cannot accept him, because it neither sees him nor knows him. But you know him, for he lives with you and will be in you. I will not leave you as orphans; I will come to you."
– John 14:12-18

"But the Advocate, the Holy Spirit, whom the Father will send in my name, will teach you all things and will remind you of everything I have said to you." – John 14:26

"When the Advocate comes, whom I will send to you from the Father—the Spirit of truth who goes out from the Father—he will testify about me. And you also must testify, for you have been with me from the beginning." – John 15:26-27

"When you are brought before synagogues, rulers and authorities, do not worry about how you will defend yourselves or what you will say, for the Holy Spirit will teach you at that time what you should say." – Luke 12:11-12

"He told them, 'This is what is written: The Messiah will suffer and rise from the dead on the third day, and repentance for the forgiveness of sins will be preached in his name to all nations, beginning at Jerusalem. You are witnesses of these things. I am going to send you what my Father has promised; but stay in the city until you have been clothed with power from on high.' " – Luke 24:46-49

We don't know at this point exactly what the disciples were thinking or feeling, but it appears they still did not totally understand what Jesus was telling them. His actual departure on what we call Ascension Day must have only added to their confusion and uncertainty. As Jesus ascended, he took the opportunity to address them one last time:

"On one occasion, while he was eating with them, he gave them this command: 'Do not leave Jerusalem, but wait for the gift my Father promised, which you have heard me speak about. For John baptized with water, but in a few days you will be baptized with the Holy Spirit.' So when they met together, they asked him, 'Lord, are you at this time going to restore the kingdom to Israel?' He said to them: 'It is not for you to know the times or dates the Father has set by his own authority. But you will receive power when the Holy Spirit comes on you; and you will be my witnesses in Jerusalem, and in all Judea and Samaria, and to the ends of the earth.' " – Acts 1:4-8

Just as Jesus instructed, the disciples returned to Jerusalem and waited. It was the time of Pentecost, a Jewish harvest festival requiring Jews to gather in Jerusalem for thanksgiving and worship. People came from many different countries, speaking many different languages, to take part in the celebration. At that time, a group of 120 believers in the risen Christ, including the eleven remaining disciples, gathered in one place. Acts 2:1-28 tells of how the promised Holy Spirit came upon these believers, giving them a spiritual gift for speaking in other languages. The believers preached in these foreign languages throughout the city that day. Foreigners staying in Jerusalem heard the disciples speaking in their own languages about the mighty works of God. Three thousand people heard God's message and believed also. The church was born.

Followers of Christ received gifts of the Holy Spirit once they accepted Christ as their Savior. References to these spiritual gifts appear throughout the rest of the New Testament. Some believers were given the message of wisdom, some leadership, some the gift of encouragement, and so on. They each served the rest of the community of believers in accordance with their individual gifts, together meeting the needs of all and glorifying God.

Somehow over the ages, this church model in which all Christians used their gifts and shared the work of the church with the Bible as their guide was discarded. Instead, church leaders held most of the power, authority, and responsibility. Many abuses took place as the church fell prey to lust for power and wealth.

The Protestant Reformation, which reached a peak with Martin Luther and John Calvin in the sixteenth century, was built around three core beliefs:

- The Bible is the primary authority.
- Justification comes through faith and the grace of God, not through human works.
- All believers are priests, or ministers, for and within God's kingdom.

While the first two core beliefs brought about change to the church, the third element was not fully realized. The belief in the priesthood of all believers impacted our views regarding our access to God. We don't need an intermediary to go to God on our behalf. We can speak directly to God. However, the implications of the priesthood of all believers were never carried through far enough regarding laypersons and a gift-based ministry. The Reformers talked about the priesthood of all believers and equipping the saints, but these principles were not widely practiced.

Across the world today, there is a movement to bring the church back to a gifts-based ministry model. This is not a new trend or fad; this is restoring God's church to God's perfect plan. By reviving gifts-based ministry, with every believer being a minister, the church is better equipped to achieve the Great Commission of Matthew 28:19, *"Therefore go and make disciples of all nations. . . ."* Every spiritual gift is designed to equip us to fulfill the Great Commission. As Christians, we are responsible for carrying on Christ's *many parts;*

work. God has given us gifts, empowering us to serve one another and glorify God.

Four foundational Bible passages guide us in thinking about spiritual gifts: 1 Corinthians 12; Romans 12:1-8; Ephesians 4:1-16; and 1 Peter 4:9-11. From these four passages we gather much of what we know about spiritual gifts. We've pulled out some key portions of these passages, which set the context for spiritual gifts. Let's stop here and consider what the Bible has to say.

Read each of the listed Bible references and follow the instructions.

1 Corinthians 12

[1]Now about the gifts of the Spirit, brothers and sisters, I do not want you to be uninformed. [2]You know that when you were pagans, somehow or other you were influenced and led astray to mute idols. [3]Therefore I want you to know that no one who is speaking by the Spirit of God says, "Jesus be cursed," and no one can say, "Jesus is Lord," except by the Holy Spirit.

[4]There are different kinds of gifts, but the same Spirit distributes them. [5]There are different kinds of service, but the same Lord. [6]There are different kinds of working, but in all of them and in everyone it is the same God at work.

[7]Now to each one the manifestation of the Spirit is given for the common good. [8]To one there is given through the Spirit a message of wisdom, to another a message of knowledge by means of the same Spirit, [9]to another faith by the same Spirit, to another gifts of healing by that one Spirit, [10]to another miraculous powers, to another prophecy, to another distinguishing between spirits, to another speaking in different kinds of tongues, and to still another the interpretation of tongues. [11]All these are the work of one and the same Spirit, and he distributes them to each one, just as he determines.

[12]Just as a body, though one, has many parts, but all its many parts form one body, so it is with Christ. [13]For we were all baptized by one Spirit so as to form one body—whether Jews or Gentiles, slave or free—and we were all given the one Spirit to drink. [14]Even so the body is not made up of one part but of many.

[15]Now if the foot should say, "Because I am not a hand, I do not belong to the body," it would not for that reason cease to be part of the body. [16]And if the ear should say, "Because I am not an eye, I do not belong to the body," it would not for that reason cease to be part of the body. [17]If the whole body were an eye, where would the sense of hearing be? If the whole body

one body

were an ear, where would the sense of smell be? ¹⁸But in fact God has placed the parts in the body, every one of them, just as he wanted them to be. ¹⁹If they were all one part, where would the body be? ²⁰As it is, there are many parts, but one body.

²¹The eye cannot say to the hand, "I don't need you!" And the head cannot say to the feet, "I don't need you!" ²²On the contrary, those parts of the body that seem to be weaker are indispensable, ²³and the parts that we think are less honorable we treat with special honor. And the parts that are unpresentable are treated with special modesty, ²⁴while our presentable parts need no special treatment. But God has put the body together, giving greater honor to the parts that lacked it, ²⁵so that there should be no division in the body, but that its parts should have equal concern for each other. ²⁶If one part suffers, every part suffers with it; if one part is honored, every part rejoices with it.

²⁷Now you are the body of Christ, and each one of you is a part of it. ²⁸And God has placed in the church first of all apostles, second prophets, third teachers, then miracles, then gifts of healing, of helping, of guidance, and of different kinds of tongues. ²⁹Are all apostles? Are all prophets? Are all teachers? Do all work miracles? ³⁰Do all have gifts of healing? Do all speak in tongues? Do all interpret? ³¹Now eagerly desire the greater gifts. And yet I will show you the most excellent way.

1. **According to verse 1, what is Paul's desire regarding the subject of spiritual gifts?**

2. **List and explain the contrasts found in verses 4-6. Hint: Look for the word *but*. Who do you see at work here?**

3. **According to verse 7, who receives the spiritual gifts, and for what purpose?**

4. **What do verses 8-11 have to say about the giving of gifts?**

5. What analogy does Paul use with respect to gifts in verses 12-17? What does this analogy illustrate? Why do you think Paul chose to use it?

6. Who determines our place in the body of Christ according to verse 18?

7. What do we learn about the individual members of the body from verses 19-24?

8. What is being said in verses 25-27 about our responsibility toward one another?

9. We learned in verses 8-11 that a variety of gifts are given. According to verses 28-30, is there any gift that is received by every member? (This is kind of a tricky question. Based on the way the questions are posed in the passage in the original Greek, the assumed answer to each of them is "no.")

different gifts

While it is good to turn to the Bible for information, we should also let the Bible form us inside. Open your Bible to 1 Corinthians 13, and take a moment to prepare yourself to be in prayer over the next five minutes or so. Slowly, prayerfully, read 1 Corinthians 13:4-7. Let it be your prayer. Conclude by asking God for help in being more loving in all that you do.

Romans 12:1-8

[1]Therefore, I urge you, brothers and sisters, in view of God's mercy, to offer your bodies as a living sacrifice, holy and pleasing to God—this is true worship. [2]Do not conform to the pattern of this world, but be transformed by the renewing of your mind. Then you will be able to test and approve what God's will is—his good, pleasing and perfect will.

[3]For by the grace given me I say to every one of you: Do not think of yourself more highly than you ought, but rather think of yourself with sober judgment, in accordance with the faith God has distributed to each of you. [4]For just as each of us has one body with many members, and these members do not all have the same function, [5]so in Christ we, though many, form one body, and each member belongs to all the others. [6]We have different gifts, according to the grace given to each of us. If your gift is prophesying, then prophesy in accordance with your faith; [7]if it is serving, then serve; if it is teaching, then teach; [8]if it is to encourage, then give encouragement; if it is giving, then give generously; if it is to lead, do it diligently; if it is to show mercy, do it cheerfully.

1. What principles might Paul be trying to get across in verses 1-3?

2. According to verse 1, offering ourselves to God is true worship. How is using our spiritual gifts in service to God "true worship"?

3. What analogy does Paul reference again in verses 4-5? Why? What's his point?

4. According to verse 6, who receives the gifts?

If you like drawing, try your hand at depicting Paul's use of the human body as an analogy for the variety of spiritual gifts.

"We have different gifts, according to the grace given to each of us." –Romans 12:6

5. What do we learn about exercising our gifts from verses 6-8?

Ephesians 4:1-7, 11-16

¹As a prisoner for the Lord, then, I urge you to live a life worthy of the calling you have received. ²Be completely humble and gentle; be patient, bearing with one another in love. ³Make every effort to keep the unity of the Spirit through the bond of peace. ⁴There is one body and one Spirit, just as you were called to one hope when you were called; ⁵one Lord, one faith, one baptism; ⁶one God and Father of all, who is over all and through all and in all.

⁷But to each one of us grace has been given as Christ apportioned it. . . .

¹¹So Christ himself gave the apostles, the prophets, the evangelists, the pastors and teachers, ¹²to equip his people for works of service, so that the body of Christ may be built up ¹³until we all reach unity in the faith and in the knowledge of the Son of God and become mature, attaining to the whole measure of the fullness of Christ.

¹⁴Then we will no longer be infants, tossed back and forth by the waves, and blown here and there by every wind of teaching and by the cunning and craftiness of people in their deceitful scheming. ¹⁵Instead, speaking the truth in love, we will in all things grow up into him who is the head, that is, Christ. ¹⁶From him the whole body, joined and held together by every supporting ligament, grows and builds itself up in love, as each part does its work.

1. What are the instructions given in verse 1-3?

2. What are the seven characteristics of all believers according to verses 4-6? What is the significance of this?

3. Who receives the gifts according to verse 7?

4. For what purpose are gifts given according to verses 11-13?

5. What are the results in verses 14-16?

1 Peter 4:9-11

⁹Offer hospitality to one another without grumbling. ¹⁰Each of you should use whatever gift you have received to serve others, as faithful stewards of God's grace in its various forms. ¹¹If you speak, you should do so as one who speaks the very words of God. If you serve, you should do so with the strength God provides, so that in all things God may be praised through Jesus Christ. To him be the glory and the power for ever and ever. Amen.

1. What spiritual gift is listed in verse 9?

2. Who receives spiritual gifts, according to verse 10?

3. How are spiritual gifts to be used?

4. What are the two categories of gifts found in this passage?

"Each of you should use whatever gift you have received to serve others."
–1 Peter 4:10

List the spiritual gifts you find in each of the Bible passages:

1 Corinthians 12:8-10, 28-30	Romans 12:1-8	Ephesians 4:1-16	1 Peter 4:9-11

So far along our journey we've learned much about the broad biblical context for spiritual gifts. The focus now turns to us as unique individuals and how what we've learned applies to us. It's time to start the process of discovering the particular gifts God has given to each one of us.

See page 23 to complete the Spiritual Gifts Discovery Tool or visit
http://ministrymatters.agroupmail.com/spiritualgifts.

Once you have finished the assessment, go to Chapter 2 and refer to the definitions and descriptions of the three gifts for which you scored the highest number. These are the gifts you should explore first.

SPIRITUAL GIFTS DISCOVERY TOOL

The following is a list of 85 statements. Before considering these, make sure you have set aside an uninterrupted time of quiet. Begin this time with prayer, and ask the Holy Spirit to guide you. Answer based on how true these statements are of your life experience, both past and present, not as you wish you would be. Remember, God's choice of gifts for you is in harmony with God's perfect plan and will for your life.

Record your answers on the line next to each statement. When you are finished, transfer your responses onto the response form. Score each one as follows:

4. Very true of me, consistently.
3. Frequently true of me.
2. Occasionally true of me.
1. Infrequently true of me.
0. Rarely, or never true of me.

___4___ 1) I am organized and detail-oriented.

___3___ 2) I would enjoy starting a church or ministry in a foreign country or culture.

___2___ 3) I can sense when someone's motives or intentions are inconsistent with the teachings of Scripture.

___2___ 4) I encourage people who are struggling in their faith through speaking, writing, artwork, singing, or prayer.

___2___ 5) I am open about my personal faith and look for opportunities to talk about it.

___1___ 6) I am confident that God will keep God's promises and act accordingly.

___3___ 7) I enjoy sharing my material blessings with others.

___3___ 8) ~~From time to time~~, my prayers for healing on behalf of others are answered in amazing or miraculous ways.

___4___ 9) I find fulfillment through performing behind-the-scenes deeds that support ministries.

___2___ 10) I enjoy making new friends, and do so easily.

___1___ 11) I enjoy studying my Bible in depth, sometimes using study tools like concordances and commentaries.

___3___ 12) People often come to me seeking guidance and direction.

___3___ 13) My heart goes out to people who are hurting, and I am moved to action.

___3___ 14) I am concerned about the spiritual growth of people I know.

___1___ 15) I confront individuals and groups who have gotten off-track and encourage them to look to God for direction.

___1___ 16) I am able to explain biblical teachings in ways that others can relate and apply to their lives.

___3___ 17) People often ask me for insight and guidance on difficult decisions or situations.

___3___ 18) I enjoy planning and organizing events or projects.

___3___ 19) I am skilled at overseeing multiple projects at once.

___1___ 20) I know when a statement or doctrine is not in line with, or contradicts, God's word.

___2___ 21) I am able to gently influence people in a way that helps them remain faithful.

___0___ 22) I often invite people to come to church, or church events, with me.

___1___ 23) I don't lose faith when bad things happen, because I know God walks beside us in all circumstances.

___3___ 24) I have ample income and give a significant portion to charitable causes.

___4___ 25) The Holy Spirit prompts me to pray for specific people who are in need and are hurting.

___3___ 26) I enjoy using my talents and skills to help various ministries.

___3___ 27) I am able to make people feel welcome and comfortable.

___0___ 28) When someone is confused, I am able to point out a Scripture passage that guides them through the issue.

___2___ 29) I provide inspiration and direction in the work of ministry and support others to accomplish the ministry's goals.

___3___ 30) I desire to follow the example of Jesus, reaching out to people in need with compassion.

___2___ 31) Sometimes I develop long-term relationships with others and nurture them in their faith walk.

___1___ 32) I see things in society that are opposed to God's will or plan, and feel led to expose them.

___3___ 33) I enjoy preparing and organizing material in order to teach it to others.

7? ___2___ 34) The solutions I provide to complex situations are always consistent with biblical truth as found in Scripture.

___3___ 35) I easily outline and implement the steps needed to achieve a vision.

___4___ 36) I like to empower others to assume leadership roles.

___2___ 37) I have been able to call the focus of individuals and groups back to the Holy Spirit and God's word.

___1___ 38) I bring comfort to people through sharing God's promises.

___0___ 39) I can share the gospel in relevant, meaningful ways.

___3___ 40) I am able to provide reassurance and encouragement to individuals or groups when they get discouraged and are ready to give up.

___2___ 41) When I see someone in need, I will share whatever I have with him or her.

___2___ 42) I believe that God answers my prayers for miraculous healings.

___2___ 43) I often help out around the church by doing "whatever needs to be done."

___2___ 44) I enjoy entertaining others in my home.

___1___ 45) I like to share with others what I have learned through studying the Bible.

___4___ 46) I encourage others to develop their skills and abilities.

___2___ 47) I enjoy visiting people who are sick or lonely to be present with them and bring them a little cheer.

_3_ 48) I enjoy teaching individuals and groups over extended periods of time versus one-time or short-term events.

_4_ 49) The Holy Spirit urges me to share what I believe God would think or say in order to encourage or guide people.

_2_ 50) Whenever I learn something new, I am thinking about how I might share the new knowledge with others.

_3_ 51) I sometimes bring clarity to difficult situations and can help point others toward God's will.

_2_ 52) I am skilled at gathering and managing the resources needed for a ministry in order for it to function properly.

_0_ 53) I am drawn to proclaim and teach the good news of the gospel in places where it has not been heard or taught.

_1_ 54) I sometimes sense the presence of evil.

_0_ 55) People are motivated to make faith-informed decisions or changes in their lives after spending time with me.

_0_ 56) I intentionally develop relationships with non-Christians for the purpose of sharing my faith.

_4_ 57) I believe God listens to and answers all prayers.

_4_ 58) I believe I have been blessed with abundant resources so that I can be a blessing to others.

_1_ 59) I am drawn to worship experiences where prayers and anointing for healing are experienced.

_3_ 60) I enjoy providing practical assistance to meet ministry needs.

_2_ 61) I am a warm, friendly person and enjoy making new people feel included in my groups or conversations.

_1_ 62) I am able to speak and teach an understanding of God and the Bible that helps others grow in faith.

_3_ 63) I often find myself in a leadership role as others look to me for leadership.

_4_ 64) I am a good listener, and people often talk to me about their troubles.

_2_ 65) I feel the responsibility of caring for the people I teach about God and God's Word.

_1_ 66) I am often led to challenge people who are heading in a harmful direction and to help them get back on a Spirit-led path.

_0_ 67) People often thank me for helping them better understand the Bible or materials from a Bible study.

_3_ 68) I am able to share words and insights that bring peaceful solutions to problems.

_3_ 69) I like to work with issues involving systems, structures, and procedures.

_0_ 70) I feel compelled to share the gospel and spend time in prayer and God's Word to prepare myself.

_3_ 71) I have experienced, personally and in groups, guidance from the Holy Spirit in answer to a time of prayer.

_2_ 72) I am led to encourage people in their faith through action.

_0_ 73) I am comfortable using prayer and Scripture to lead people to Christ.

_3_ 74) I approach challenges with confidence when I believe I am following the will of God.

_3_ 75) Everything I have is a gift from God and I seek out ways to share those gifts with others.

_2_ 76) People have shared tangible ways in which they have experienced God's healing touch as a result of my prayers on their behalf.

_2_ 77) Serving God through simple tasks is something I find rewarding.

_1_ 78) I often serve as host or hostess for group functions, either in my home or at other locations.

_0_ 79) God sometimes gives me a special insight into God's Word that enables me to teach others in a way that helps them understand.

_2_ 80) I tend to have a "big picture" perspective and can clearly communicate vision in a way that is understandable and motivating.

_3_ 81) I can minister to people in need in a way that protects their dignity.

_2_ 82) I am not only interested in instructing people about God, but also care about their restoration and relationship with God.

_2_ 83) God's word and /or will sometimes come to mind in situations where people need challenge or encouragement.

_1_ 84) I look for opportunities to share what I have learned about the Bible.

_4_ 85) The Holy Spirit provides me with spiritual thoughts and words to share to help bring focus and clarity in times of conflict or disorder.

Place your score for each of the statements on the appropriate line below. Transfer your totals to the Spiritual Gifts list on page 29.

4. — Very true of me, consistently.
3. — Frequently true of me.
2. — Occasionally true of me.
1. — Infrequently true of me.
0. — Rarely, or never true of me.

Total your responses across.   TOTAL

1 _4_ 18 _3_ 35 _3_ 52 _2_ 69 _3_ A _15_

2 _3_ 19 _3_ 36 _4_ 53 _0_ 70 _0_ B _10_

3 _2_ 20 _1_ 37 _2_ 54 _1_ 71 _3_ C _9_

4 _2_ 21 _2_ 38 _1_ 55 _0_ 72 _2_ D _7_

5 _2_ 22 _0_ 39 _0_ 56 _0_ 73 _0_ E _2_

6 _1_ 23 _1_ 40 _3_ 57 _4_ 74 _3_ F _12_

Total your responses across.   TOTAL

7 _3_   24 _3_ 41 _2_ 58 _4_ 75 _3_ G _15_

8 _3_   25 _4_ 42 _2_ 59 _1_ 76 _2_ H _12_

9 _4_   26 _3_ 43 _2_ 60 _3_ 77 _2_ I _14_

10 _2_ 27 _3_ 44 _2_ 61 _2_ 78 _1_ J _10_

11 _1_ 28 _0_ 45 _1_ 62 _1_ 79 _0_ K _3_

12 _3_ 29 _2_ 46 _4_ 63 _3_ 80 _2_ L _14_

13 _3_ 30 _3_ 47 _2_ 64 _4_ 81 _3_ M _15_

14 _3_ 31 _2_ 48 _3_ 65 _2_ 82 _2_ N _12_

15 _1_ 32 _1_ 49 _4_ 66 _1_ 83 _2_ O _9_

16 _1_ 33 _3_ 50 _2_ 67 _0_ 84 _1_ P _7_

17 _3_ 34 _2_ 51 _3_ 68 _3_ 85 _4_ Q _15_

SPIRITUAL GIFTS	TOTAL SCORE
A. Administration (Guidance)....	(15)
B. Apostleship......................	10
C. Distinguishing of Spirits........	9
D. Encouragement...................	7
E. Evangelism.......................	2
F. Faith..............................	12
G. Giving............................	(15)
H. Healing...........................	12
I. Helps (Serving)...................	(14)
J. Hospitality	10
K. Message of Knowledge........	3
L. Leadership........................	(14)
M. Mercy............................	(15)
N. Pastor-Teacher (Shepherding)..	12
O. Prophecy.........................	9
P. Teaching.........................	7
Q. Message of Wisdom...........	(15)

Please circle yes / no whether you have these self-evident spiritual gifts:

R. Miraculous Powers........... Yes / (No)

S. Speaking in Tongues......... Yes / (No)

T. Interpretation of Tongues... Yes / (No)

My top three gifts, according to my scores, are:

1. ___Administration (Guidance)___

2. ___Giving___

3. ___Mercy___

4. ___Message of Wisdom___

5. ___Helps (Serving)___

6. ___Leadership___

Spiritual Gifts

Holy Spirit

CHAPTER 2

Spiritual Gifts Defined

*Each of you should use whatever gift you have received
to serve others, as faithful stewards of God's grace
in its various forms.—1 Peter 4:10*

Let's talk for a moment about the definition of spiritual gifts . . .

> Spiritual gifts are special (divine) abilities given to every Christian, by the grace of God, through the Holy Spirit, to be used to serve and strengthen one another, and to glorify God.

So, in a nutshell, spiritual gifts are:

- Divine abilities (not something you've learned)
- Given to every Christian (yes, even YOU)
- Given through the grace of God (not something you've earned)
- Given by the Holy Spirit (God chooses which gift(s) you receive)
- Used to serve and strengthen one another (to build each other up, not yourself)
- Used to glorify God (for God's purposes, to God's glory)

It's important to note a few things about the scriptural context for spiritual gifts.

1) There are differences of opinion among biblical scholars regarding the giving of spiritual gifts. Some believe that every human is born with his or her spiritual gifts, and they

"You are naturally drawn to do what God has equipped you to do."

become activated by the Holy Spirit when a person accepts Christ. Others believe that Scripture clearly says the gifts are distributed only after a person accepts Christ. We are not here to argue either side, only to make sure you know that spiritual gifts ARE scriptural.

2) Experts also disagree about the number of gifts and what they are. Some lists of gifts number only seven gifts, others up to thirty. Here is our position on that: Nowhere in the Bible do we see the words: "And thus saith the Lord, 'This is a complete and final listing of the spiritual gifts.' " We've included the passages that we feel are indisputably referring to spiritual gifts, and our list includes the gifts mentioned specifically in those passages. Quite frankly, if we're arguing about how many "real" spiritual gifts there are, we're missing the point. The point of spiritual gifts is to DO what you are uniquely gifted to do to serve others and glorify God. If you are uniquely gifted to dance, and you use that gift for those purposes, that's fantastic. If you believe you have a gift of hospitality, and use that gift to make others welcome in the body of Christ, that's perfect, too.

By now, you should have prayerfully considered the questions within the Spiritual Gifts Discovery Tool (see pages 23-29) and possibly identified your top three spiritual gifts. Written assessments are meant to be helpful tools that assist you in narrowing down the possibilities and allowing you to focus on a few of the spiritual gifts we enumerate here. Confirmation that you have a certain spiritual gift may come in a variety of ways:

• You will be drawn to use your spiritual gift(s). You are naturally drawn to do what God has equipped you to do.
• Others will recognize gift(s) in you. They are benefiting.
• You will be comfortable serving in your area of spiritual gifting. This doesn't mean you won't have butterflies!
• You will be effective when you exercise your gift(s). God gets the glory.

Let's continue this journey. Our path is leading us to a deeper understanding of each of the spiritual gifts. Read over the Scriptures associated with each spiritual gift. The Bible is rich with truth for us. The Holy Spirit is our teacher and our guide to understanding what God wants us to know.

In the section that follows, we've provided a list of spiritual gifts referred to in the Bible. A transliteration of the Greek word used in the New Testament for the spiritual gift is given,

guidance

followed by a definition. Then we offer our best understanding of the spiritual gift. Scripture passages that mention each spiritual gift, or show the gift in action, are given, followed by space for you to reflect on where and how you see each specific spiritual gift at work around you or within you today.

ADMINISTRATION (GUIDANCE)

Greek: kybernēsis = pilotage, to steer, a guide, directorship in the church

The spiritual gift of Administration (or Guidance) is the God-given ability to organize and manage information, people, events, and resources to accomplish the objectives of a ministry. People with this gift handle details carefully and thoroughly. They are skilled in determining priorities, and in planning and directing the steps needed to achieve a goal. They feel frustrated when faced with disorder, and are uncomfortable with inefficiency. People with the gift of Administration often make it easier for others to use their own gifts, simply by keeping things organized and flowing smoothly.

Scripture References

"And God has placed in the church first of all apostles, second prophets, third teachers, then miracles, then gifts of healing, of helping, of guidance, and of different kinds of tongues."
– 1 Corinthians 12:28

"In those days when the number of disciples was increasing, the Hellenistic Jews among them complained against the Hebraic Jews because their widows were being overlooked in the daily distribution of food. So the Twelve gathered all the disciples together and said, 'It would not be right for us to neglect the ministry of the word of God in order to wait on tables. Brothers and sisters, choose seven men from among you who are known to be full of the Spirit and wisdom. We will turn this responsibility over to them and will give our attention to prayer and the ministry of the word.'

"This proposal pleased the whole group. They chose Stephen, a man full of faith and of the Holy Spirit; also Philip, Procorus, Nicanor, Timon, Parmenas, and Nicolas from Antioch, a convert to Judaism. They presented them to the apostles, who prayed and laid their hands on them. So the word of God spread. The number of disciples in Jerusalem increased rapidly, and a large number of priests became obedient to the faith." – Acts 6:1-7

building new churches or ministries

"The reason I left you in Crete was that you might put in order what was left unfinished and appoint elders in every town, as I directed you." – Titus 1:5

- Examples of use today:

- Do you know anyone who has the gift of Administration? How can you encourage them as they exercise their spiritual gift?

- Do you believe you have the spiritual gift of Administration? Why?

APOSTLESHIP

Greek: apostolos = a delegate, a special ambassador of the gospel, officially a commissioner of Christ, a messenger, one who is sent

The divine ability to build the foundation of new churches by preaching the word, teaching others to live by Christ's commandments through the example of their own lives, and preparing the people to serve one another. Persons with the gift of Apostleship are not only eager to bring the gospel to those who have never heard it; they prepare those people to continue the work after they have left. They enthusiastically approach new ministries, churches, or settings, and realize the need to adapt methods of evangelism and service to widely different environments. People with this gift might envision themselves as missionaries, but some may not—they may instead accept and exercise leadership over a number of new churches or ministries.

Scripture References

"So Christ himself gave the apostles, the prophets, the evangelists, the pastors and teachers, to equip his people for works of service, so that the body of Christ may be built up until we all reach unity in the faith and in the knowledge of the Son of God and become mature, attaining to the whole measure of the fullness of Christ." – Ephesians 4:11-13

"You know brothers and sisters, that our visit to you was not without results. We had previously suffered and been treated outrageously in Philippi, as you know, but with the help of our God we dared to tell you his gospel in the face of strong opposition. For the appeal we make does not spring from error or impure motives, nor are we trying to trick you. On the contrary, we speak as those approved by God to be entrusted with the gospel. We are not trying to please people but God, who tests our hearts. You know we never used flattery, nor did we put on a mask to cover up greed—God is our witness. We were not looking for praise from any human being, not from you or anyone else, even though as apostles of Christ we could have asserted our prerogatives. Instead, we were like young children among you.

"Just as a nursing mother cares for her children, so we cared for you. Because we loved you so much, we were delighted to share with you not only the gospel of God, but our lives as well. Surely you remember, brothers and sisters, our toil and hardship; we worked night and day in order not to be a burden to anyone while we preached the gospel of God to you.

"You are our witnesses, and so is God, of how holy, righteous, and blameless we were among you who believed. For you know that we dealt with each of you as a father deals with his own children, encouraging, comforting, and urging you to live lives worthy of God, who calls you into his kingdom and glory." – 1 Thessalonians 2:1-12

"I want you to recall the words spoken in the past by the holy prophets and the command given by our Lord and Savior through your apostles." – 2 Peter 3:2

- Examples of use today:

- Do you know anyone who has the gift of Apostleship? How can you encourage them as they exercise their spiritual gift?

- Do you believe you have the spiritual gift of Apostleship? Why?

DISTINGUISHING OF SPIRITS

Greek: diakrisis = judicial estimation, discerning pneuma = a current of air, figuratively "a spirit," mental disposition

The divine ability to recognize what is of God and what is not of God—to distinguish between good and evil, truth and error, and pure motives and impure motives. People with this gift usually can rely on instincts or first impressions to tell when a person or message is deceptive or inconsistent with biblical truths. They can sense the presence of evil, and they question motives, intentions, doctrine, deeds, and beliefs. These

— read people —

people must take care to use their gift in a way that brings good to the body of Christ—to judge with mercy and understanding rather than to condemn. It is unfortunate that people sometimes use this gift as a weapon against someone they disagree with, as opposed to seeking to understand whether their feeling is truly Spirit led.

Scripture References

"Dear friends, do not believe every spirit, but test the spirits to see whether they are from God, because many false prophets have gone out into the world." – 1 John 4:1

"As soon as it was night, the believers sent Paul and Silas away to Berea. On arriving there, they went to the Jewish synagogue. Now the Berean Jews were of more noble character than those in Thessalonica, for they received the message with great eagerness and examined the Scriptures every day to see if what Paul said was true. Many of them believed, as did also a number of prominent Greek women and many Greek men." – Acts 17:10-12

"They traveled through the whole island until they came to Paphos. There they met a Jewish sorcerer and false prophet named Bar-Jesus, who was an attendant of the proconsul, Sergius Paulus. The proconsul, an intelligent man, sent for Barnabas and Saul because he wanted to hear the word of God. But Elymas the sorcerer (for that is what his name means) opposed them and tried to turn the proconsul from the faith. Then Saul, who was also called Paul, filled with the Holy Spirit, looked straight at Elymas and said, 'You are a child of the devil and an enemy of everything that is right! You are full of all kinds of deceit and trickery. Will you never stop perverting the right ways of the Lord?' " – Acts 13:6-10

- Examples of use today:

- Do you know anyone who has the gift of Distinguishing of Spirits? How can you encourage them as they exercise their spiritual gift?

- Do you believe you have the spiritual gift of Distinguishing of Spirits? Why?

discernment

ENCOURAGEMENT

Greek: paraklēsis= imploration, solace, comfort, exhortation, entreaty

The God-given ability to encourage, help, intercede for, and be an advocate for others in a way that motivates others to grow in their faith and urges them to action. Encouragement (also referred to as Exhortation) takes many forms, and can be done through personal relationships, music, writings, intercessory prayer, and speaking, to name a few. People with this gift encourage others to remain faithful, even in the midst of struggles. They are sensitive and sympathetic toward another person's emotional state and exhort selflessly, with affection, not contempt. They can see positive traits or aspects that other persons overlook and often have more faith in other persons than they have in themselves.

Scripture References

"They preached the gospel in that city and won a large number of disciples. Then they returned to Lystra, Iconium, and Antioch, strengthening the disciples and encouraging them to remain true to the faith." – Acts 14:21-22a

"So they were sent off and went down to Antioch, where they gathered the church together and delivered the letter. The people read it and were glad for its encouraging message." – Acts: 15:30-31

"In the presence of God and of Christ Jesus, who will judge the living and the dead, and in view of his appearing and his kingdom, I give you this charge: Preach the word; be prepared in season and out of season; correct, rebuke, and encourage— with great patience and careful instruction." – 2 Timothy 4:1-2

"When the uproar had ended, Paul sent for the disciples and, after encouraging them, said good-by and set out for Macedonia. He traveled through that area, speaking many words of encouragement to the people. . . ." – Acts 20:1-2

- Examples of use today:

- Do you know anyone who has the gift of Encouragement? How can you encourage them as they exercise their spiritual gift?

- Do you believe you have the spiritual gift of Encouragement? Why?

EVANGELISM

Greek: euagelistēs = a preacher of the gospel

The divine ability to spread the good news of Jesus Christ so that unknowing persons respond with faith and discipleship. Contrary to what you might think, people with the gift of Evangelism do not all speak of their faith from a podium or by taking their message door-to-door through a neighborhood, though some do. Most people with this gift simply speak comfortably about their faith; nonbelievers are drawn into this circle of comfort. These people enjoy many friendships outside of their Christian community. They enjoy helping others see how Christianity can fulfill their needs. They eagerly study questions that challenge Christianity. They respond clearly in ways that connect with individuals—meeting the individuals right where they are.

Scripture References

"Now an angel of the Lord said to Philip, 'Go south to the road—the desert road—that goes down from Jerusalem to Gaza.' So he started out, and on his way he met an Ethiopian eunuch, an important official in charge of all the treasury of the Kandake (which means the "queen of the Ethiopians"). This man had gone to Jerusalem to worship, and on his way home was sitting in his chariot reading the Book of Isaiah the prophet. The Spirit told Philip, 'Go to that chariot and stay near it.'

"Then Philip ran up to the chariot and heard the man reading Isaiah the prophet. 'Do you understand what you are reading?' Philip asked.

'How can I,' he said, 'unless someone explains it to me?' So he invited Philip to come up and sit with him.

"This is the passage of Scripture the eunuch was reading:

'He was led like a sheep to the slaughter,
And as a lamb before its shearer is silent,
So he did not open his mouth.
In his humiliation he was deprived of justice.
Who can speak of his descendants?
For his life was taken from the earth.'

"The eunuch asked Philip, 'Tell me, please, who is the prophet talking about, himself or someone else?' Then Philip began with that very passage of Scripture and told him the good news about Jesus." – Acts 8:26-35

"Paul and his companions traveled throughout the region of Phrygia and Galatia, having been kept by the Holy Spirit from preaching the word in the province of Asia. When they came to the border of Mysia, they tried to enter Bithynia, but the Spirit of Jesus would not allow them to. So they passed by Mysia and went down to Troas. During the night Paul had a vision of a man of Macedonia standing and begging him, 'Come over to Macedonia and help us.' After Paul had seen the vision, we got ready at once to leave for Macedonia, concluding that God had called us to preach the gospel to them."
– Acts 16:6-10

"Day after day, in the temple courts and from house to house, they never stopped teaching and proclaiming the good news that Jesus is the Messiah."
– Acts 5:42

"So they set out and went from village to village, proclaiming the good news and healing people everywhere." – Luke 9:6

- Examples of use today:

- Do you know anyone who has the gift of Evangelism? How can you encourage them as they exercise their spiritual gift?

- Do you believe you have the spiritual gift of Evangelism? Why?

FAITH

Greek: pistis = faith in God, a personal surrender to God with a conduct inspired by such surrender, moral conviction, assurance

The divine ability to recognize what God wants done, and to act when others fall back in doubt. Although as Christians we are all called to have faith, people with the spiritual gift of Faith receive it in an extraordinary measure. Even in the face of barriers that overwhelm others, people with this gift simply have confidence that God will see God's will done. Believing deeply in the power of prayer, they also know that God is both present and active in their lives. People with this gift, by their works and by their words, show others that God is faithful to God's promises.

Scripture References

"Jesus stepped into a boat, crossed over and came to his own town. Some men brought to him a paralyzed man, lying on a mat. When Jesus saw their faith, he said to the man, 'Take heart, son; your sins are forgiven.' " – Matthew 9:1-2

"Just then a woman who had been subject to bleeding for twelve years came up behind him and touched the edge of his cloak. She said to herself, 'If I only touch his cloak, I will be healed.'

"Jesus turned and saw her. 'Take heart, daughter,' he said, 'your faith has healed you.' " – Matthew 9:20-22

"But you, man of God, flee from all this, and pursue righteousness, godliness, faith, love, endurance and gentleness. Fight the good fight of faith. Take hold of the eternal life to which you were called when you made your good confession in the presence of many witnesses."
– 1 Timothy 6:11-12

"For it is by grace you have been saved, through faith—and this is not from yourselves, it is the gift of God—not by works, so that no one can boast. For we are God's handiwork, created in Christ Jesus to do good works, which God prepared in advance for us to do." – Ephesians 2:8-10

". . . strengthening the disciples and encouraging them to remain true to the faith." – Acts 14:22a

- Examples of use today:

- Do you know anyone who has the gift of Faith? How can you encourage them as they exercise their spiritual gift?

- Do you believe you have the spiritual gift of Faith? Why?

generous

GIVING

Greek: metadidōmi = to give over, share, impart

The God-given ability to give material wealth freely and joyfully, knowing that spiritual wealth will abound as God's work is advanced. Those with the gift of Giving are not always affluent but are always generous with what they DO have. People with this gift usually manage their finances well, may have a special ability to make money, and tend to be frugal in their lifestyle. They use these skills to increase their support for God's work, and trust that God will provide for their needs. They are often comfortable and successful in approaching others for gifts. Instead of asking, "How much of my money do I give to God?" they ask, "How much of God's money do I keep?"

Scripture References

"John answered, 'Anyone who has two shirts should share with the one who has none, and anyone who has food should do the same.' " – Luke 3:11

". . . if it is to encourage, then give encouragement; if it is giving, then give generously; if it is to lead, do it diligently; if it is to show mercy, do it cheerfully."
– Romans 12:8

". . . so we cared for you. Because we loved you so much, we were delighted to share with you not only the gospel of God but our lives as well."
– 1 Thessalonians 2:8

"Jesus sat down opposite the place where the offerings were put and watched the crowd putting their money into the temple treasury. Many rich people threw in large amounts. But a poor widow came and put in two very small copper coins, worth only a fraction of a penny.

"Calling his disciples to him, Jesus said, 'Truly I tell you, this poor widow has put more into the treasury than all the others. They gave out of their wealth; but she, out of her poverty, put in everything— all she had to live on.' " – Mark 12:41-44

- Examples of use today:

- Do you know anyone who has the gift of Giving? How can you encourage them as they exercise their spiritual gift?

- Do you believe you have the spiritual gift of Giving? Why?

HEALING

Greek: charisma = a spiritual endowment, a divine gratuity, a religious qualification
iama = cures, healings

The divine ability to bring wholeness—physical, emotional, or spiritual—to others. People with this gift listen skillfully as they seek God's guidance to learn the needs of the sick and to determine the causes and nature of an illness. They believe that God can cure and that prayer can overcome any negative forces at work (but they also recognize that God might have a different plan). Their tools include prayer, touch, and spoken words. This gift shows God's power; at the same time, it is to God's glory. The goal of healing is not just healing itself, but spreading the gospel by pointing to the power of Jesus Christ and to show the glory of God.

Scripture References

"Jesus went throughout Galiliee teaching in their synagogues, proclaiming the good news of the kingdom, and healing every disease and sickness among the people." – Matthew 4:23

"He welcomed them and spoke to them about the kingdom of God, and healed those who needed healing."
– Luke 9:11b

"You know what has happened throughout the province of Judea, beginning in Galilee after the baptism that John preached—how God anointed Jesus of Nazareth with the Holy Spirit and power, and how he went around doing good and healing all who were under the power of the devil, because God was with him."
– Acts 10:37-38

"God did extraordinary miracles through Paul, so that even handkerchiefs and aprons that had touched him were taken to the sick, and their illnesses were cured and the evil spirits left them."
– Acts 19:11-12

• Examples of use today:

• Do you know anyone who has the gift of Healing? How can you encourage them as they exercise their spiritual gift?

• Do you believe you have the spiritual gift of Healing? Why?

performing practical tasks to meet needs

HELPS (Serving)

Greek: diakonia = attendance, aid, relief, service, ministry

The God-given ability to work along-side others in performing practical and often behind-the-scenes tasks to sustain and enhance the body of Christ. A person with this gift receives spiritual satisfaction from doing everyday necessary tasks; he or she may prefer to work quietly and without public recognition. When a need is seen, the helper frequently takes care of it without being asked. The helper's work often frees up other persons so that they may carry out their own ministries.

Scripture References

"God is not unjust; he will not forget your work and the love you have shown him as you have helped his people and continue to help them." – Hebrews 6:10

"Only Luke is with me. Get Mark and bring him with you, because he is helpful to me in my ministry." – 2 Timothy 4:11

"Then Felix, who was well acquainted with the Way, adjourned the proceedings. 'When Lysias the commander comes,' he said, 'I will decide your case.' He ordered the centurion to keep Paul under guard but to give him some freedom and permit his friends to take care of his needs."
– Acts 24:22-23

"But I think it is necessary to send back to you Epaphroditus, my brother, co-worker, and fellow soldier, who is also your messenger, whom you sent to take care of my needs. For he longs for all of you and is distressed because you heard he was ill. Indeed he was ill, and almost died. But God had mercy on him, and not on him only but also on me, to spare me sorrow upon sorrow. Therefore I am all the more eager to send him, so that when you see him again you may be glad and I may have less anxiety. Welcome him in the Lord with great joy, and honor people like him, because he almost died for the work of Christ. He risked his life to make up for the help you your selves could not give me."
– Philippians 2:25-30

- Examples of use today:

- Do you know anyone who has the gift of Helping? How can you encourage them as they exercise their spiritual gift?

- Do you believe you have the spiritual gift of Helping? Why?

HOSPITALITY

Greek: philoxenos = fond of guests, i.e. hospitable, given to hospitality

The divine ability to make others feel welcome and comfortable. People with the gift of hospitality often love to entertain. Sometimes, however, their gift is simply demonstrated by a warm handshake or hug, a bright smile, and a tendency to greet new people and help them get acclimated to a new place or situation. People are drawn to persons with this gift—they often have many acquaintances or friends and help others make connections, too.

Scripture References

"Offer hospitality to one another without grumbling. Each of you should use whatever gift you have received to serve others, as faithful stewards of God's grace in its various forms." – 1 Peter 4:9-10

"Share with the Lord's people who are in need. Practice hospitality."
– Romans 12:13

"Since an overseer manages God's household, he must be blameless—not overbearing, not quick-tempered, not given to drunkenness, not violent, not pursuing dishonest gain. Rather, he must be hospitable, one who loves what is good, who is self-controlled, upright, holy, and disciplined." – Titus 1:7-8

"Now the overseer is to be above reproach, faithful to his wife, temperate, self-controlled, respectable, hospitable, able to teach." – 1 Timothy 3:2

- Examples of use today:

- Do you know anyone who has the gift of Hospitality? How can you encourage them as they exercise their spiritual gift?

- Do you believe you have the spiritual gift of Hospitality? Why?

making others feel welcome and comfortable

INTERPRETATION OF TONGUES

Greek: hermēneia= translation
glōssa = tongues, a language, specifically one not
naturally learned

The divine ability to translate the message of someone speaking in tongues. People who use this gift may or may not also have the gift of speaking in tongues, and they may or may not remember the message they interpret when they have finished doing so. People with this gift enable the gift of tongues to build up the church, by interpreting God's message for the people.

Scripture References

". . . to another miraculous powers, to another prophecy, to another distinguishing between spirits, to another speaking in different kinds of tongues, and to still another the interpretation of tongues."
– 1 Corinthians 12:10

"Now brothers and sisters, if I come to you and speak in tongues, what good will I be to you, unless I bring to you some revelation or knowledge or prophecy or word of instruction? Even in the case of lifeless things that make sounds, such as the pipe or harp, how will anyone know what tune is being played unless there is a distinction in the notes? Again, if the trumpet does not sound a clear call, who will get ready for battle? So it is with you. Unless you speak intelligible words with your tongue, how will anyone know what you are saying? You will just be speaking into the air. Undoubtedly there are all sorts of languages in the world, yet none of them is without meaning. If then I do not grasp the meaning of what someone is saying, I am a foreigner to the speaker, and the speaker is a foreigner to me. So it is with you. Since you are eager for gifts of the Spirit, try to excel in those that build up the church.

"For this reason those who speak in a tongue should pray that they may interpret what they say." – 1 Corinthians 14:6-13

"Everything must be done so that the church may be built up. If anyone speaks in a tongue, two—or at the most three—should speak, one at a time, and someone must interpret. If there is no interpreter, the speaker should keep quiet in the church; let them speak to themselves and to God."
– 1 Corinthians 14:26b-28

- Examples of use today:

- Do you know anyone who has the gift of Interpretation of Tongues? How can you encourage them as they exercise their spiritual gift?

- Do you believe you have the spiritual gift of Interpretation of Tongues? Why?

MESSAGE OF KNOWLEDGE

Greek: logos = something said, utterance, communication
gnōsis = knowledge

The God-given ability to understand, organize, and effectively use or communicate information to advance God's purposes. The information may come either from the Holy Spirit or from sources around us. People with this gift enjoy studying the Bible and other sources to gain facts, insights, and truths. The term "message of knowledge" is intentional. This gift is not knowledge for one's own benefit—it must be communicated and shared with others. People with this gift use their knowledge for projects, ministries, or teaching. They organize it in order to pass it to other persons for their use and benefit. The Holy Spirit appears to be at work when these people show unusual insight or understanding.

Scripture References

'The fear of the LORD is the beginning of knowledge,
"but fools despise wisdom and instruction." – Proverbs 1:7

"Then I will give you shepherds after my own heart, who will lead you with knowledge and understanding."
– Jeremiah 3:15

"For the lips of a priest ought to preserve knowledge, because he is the messenger of the LORD Almighty and people seek instruction from his mouth."
– Malachi 2:7

"For this very reason, make every effort to add to your faith goodness; and to goodness, knowledge; and to knowledge, self-control; and to self-control, perseverance; and to perseverance, godliness; and to godliness, mutual affection; and to mutual affection, love. For if you possess these qualities in increasing measure, they will keep you from being ineffective and unproductive in your knowledge of our Lord Jesus Christ." – 2 Peter 1:5-8

• Examples of use today:

• Do you know anyone who has the gift of Message of Knowledge? How can you encourage them as they exercise their spiritual gift?

• Do you believe you have the spiritual gift of Word Message of Knowledge? Why?

LEADERSHIP

Greek: proistēmi = to stand before, to preside, maintain, be over

The divine ability to motivate, coordinate, and direct people doing God's work. People with this gift are visionaries who inspire others to work together to make the vision a reality. They take responsibility for setting and achieving goals; they step in where there is a lack of direction. They build a team of talented persons, and then they empower them. These persons are called to be servant-leaders. Held to a high moral standard, they lead by the example of their own lives.

Scripture References

"Join together in following my example, brothers and sisters, and just as you have us as a model, keep your eyes on those who live as we do."
– Philippians 3:17

"When he had finished washing their feet, he put on his clothes and returned to his place. 'Do you understand what I have done for you?' he asked them. 'You call me "Teacher" and "Lord" and rightly so, for that is what I am. Now that I, your Lord and Teacher, have washed your feet, you also should wash one another's feet. I have set you an example that you should do as I have done for you.' " – John 13:12-15

"Remember your leaders, who spoke the word of God to you. Consider the outcome of their way of life and imitate their faith. . . . Have confidence in your leaders and submit to their authority, because they keep watch over you as those who must give an account. Do this so that their work will be a joy, not a burden, for that would be of no benefit to you."
– Hebrews 13:7, 17

- Examples of use today:

- Do you know anyone who has the gift of Leadership? How can you encourage them as they exercise their spiritual gift?

- Do you believe you have the spiritual gift of Leadership? Why?

servant-leader

compassion in action
MERCY

Greek: eleeō = to have compassion, to have mercy on

The God-given ability to see and feel the suffering of others and to minister to them with love and understanding. More simply, this gift is "compassion in action." People with this gift are called to reach out to someone who is hurt or rejected, easing his or her suffering. They feel fulfilled when they can show others that God loves them. They are skilled at gaining the trust of those in need and enjoy finding ways to comfort them.

Scripture References

"Jesus went through all the towns and villages, teaching in their synagogues, proclaiming the good news of the kingdom and healing every disease and sickness. When he saw the crowds, he had compassion on them, because they were harassed and helpless, like sheep without a shepherd." – Matthew 9:35-36

"On one occasion an expert in the law stood up to test Jesus. 'Teacher,' he asked, 'what must I do to inherit eternal life?'

'What is written in the Law?' he replied. 'How do you read it?'

"He answered, 'Love the Lord your God with all your heart and with all your soul and with all your strength and with all your mind'; and, 'Love your neighbor as yourself.'

'You have answered correctly,' Jesus replied. 'Do this and you will live.'

"But he wanted to justify himself, so he asked Jesus, 'And who is my neighbor?'

"In reply Jesus said: 'A man was going down from Jerusalem to Jericho, when he fell into the hands of robbers. They stripped him of his clothes, beat him and went away, leaving him half dead. A priest happened to be going down the same road, and when he saw the man, he passed by him on the other side. So too, a Levite, when he came to the place and saw him, passed by on the other side. But a Samaritan, as he traveled, came to where the man was; and when he saw him, he took pity on him. He went to him and bandaged his wounds, pouring on oil and wine. Then he put the man on his own donkey, brought him to an inn and took care of him. The next day he took out two denarii and gave them to the innkeeper. 'Look after him,' he said, 'and when I return, I will reimburse you for any extra expense you may have.'

'Which of these three do you think was a neighbor to the man who fell into the hands of robbers?'

"The expert in the law replied, 'The one who had mercy on him.'

"Jesus told him, 'Go and do likewise.' " – Luke 10:25-37

"Therefore, as God's chosen people, holy and dearly loved, clothe yourselves with compassion, kindness, humility, gentleness and patience. Bear with each other and forgive one another if any of you has a grievance against someone. Forgive as the Lord forgave you. And over all these virtues put on love, which binds them all together in perfect unity.

"Let the peace of Christ rule in your hearts, since as members of one body you were called to peace. And be thankful." – Colossians 3:12-15

- Examples of use today:

- Do you know anyone who has the gift of Mercy? How can you encourage them as they exercise their spiritual gift?

- Do you believe you have the spiritual gift of Mercy? Why?

MIRACULOUS POWERS

Greek: energēma = an effect, working, operation
dynamis = force, power, specifically miraculous power

The divine ability to perform miracles that testify to the truth of the gospel. People with this gift perform miracles (also referred to as "signs" and "wonders") among the people for the purpose of getting their attention, so as to point to the mighty works of God, testifying to the truth of the gospel in order to lead people to faith. The performance of these miracles leads to listening, following, and believing in the message by those who witness them.

Scripture References

"What Jesus did here in Cana of Galilee was the first of the signs through which he revealed his glory; and his disciples put their faith in him." – John 2:11

". . . and a great crowd of people followed him because they saw the signs he had performed by healing the sick." – John 6:2

signs and wonders

"People of Israel, listen to this: Jesus of Nazareth was a man accredited by God to you by miracles, wonders and signs, which God did among you through him, as you yourselves know." – Acts 2:22

"Those who had been scattered preached the word wherever they went. Philip went down to a city in Samaria and proclaimed the Messiah there. When the crowds heard Philip and saw the signs he performed, they all paid close attention to what he said. . . . Simon himself believed and was baptized. And he followed Philip everywhere, astonished by the great signs and miracles he saw." – Acts 8:4-6, 13

"This salvation, which was first announced by the Lord, was confirmed to us by those who heard him. God also testified to it by signs, wonders and various miracles, and by gifts of the Holy Spirit distributed according to his will."
– Hebrews 2:3b-4

- Examples of use today:

- Do you know anyone who has the gift of Miraculous Powers? How can you encourage them as they exercise their spiritual gift?

- Do you believe you have the spiritual gift of Miraculous Powers? Why?

PASTOR - TEACHER

Greek: poimēn = a shepherd
didaskalos = an instructor, master, teacher

The divine ability to guide, protect, and care for other people as they experience spiritual growth. People with this gift enjoy working with groups of people and nurturing their growth over an extended period of time. Because of these long-term relationships, they establish trust and confidence and are able to take the time to care for the "whole person." They can assess where a person is spiritually and then develop or find places where that person can continue his or her journey of faith. They model compas-

sion. The phrase for this gift in the original Greek indicates one gift—"pastor-teacher," not two gifts, "pastor" and "teacher." The primary difference between a pastor-teacher (or shepherd) and a teacher seems to be the longer-term, holistic care provided (in addition to instruction) by a shepherd, versus a teacher, who may operate in a shorter-term aspect, imparting knowledge and instruction, but not necessarily care.

Scripture References

"To the elders among you, I appeal as a fellow elder and a witness of Christ's

sufferings who also will share in the glory to be revealed: Be shepherds of God's flock that is under your care, watching over them—not because you must, but because you are willing, as God wants you to be; not pursuing dishonest gain, but eager to serve; not lording it over those entrusted to you, but being examples to the flock."
– 1 Peter 5:1-3

" 'Very truly I tell you Pharisees, anyone who does not enter the sheep pen by the gate, but climbs in by some other way, is a thief and a robber. The one who enters by the gate is the shepherd of the sheep. The gatekeeper opens the gate for him, and the sheep listen to his voice. He calls his own sheep by name and leads them out. When he has brought out all his own, he goes on ahead of them, and his sheep follow him because they know his voice. But they will never follow a stranger; in fact, they will run away from him because they do not recognize a stranger's voice.' " Jesus used this figure of speech, but the Pharisees did not understand what he was telling them.

"Therefore Jesus said again, 'Very truly I tell you, I am the gate for the sheep. All who have come before me are thieves and robbers, but the sheep have not listened to them. I am the gate; whoever enters through me will be saved. They will come in and go out, and find pasture. The thief comes only to steal and kill and destroy; I have come that they may have life, and have it to the full.

'I am the good shepherd. The good shepherd lays down his life for the sheep. The hired hand is not the shepherd and does not own the sheep. So when he sees the wolf coming, he abandons the sheep and runs away. Then the wolf attacks the flock and scatters it. The man runs away because he is a hired hand and cares nothing for the sheep.

'I am the good shepherd; I know my sheep and my sheep know me—just as the Father knows me and I know the Father— and I lay down my life for the sheep. I have other sheep that are not of this sheep pen. I must bring them also. They too will listen to my voice, and there shall be one flock and one shepherd.' " – John 10:1-16

"Then I will give you shepherds after my own heart, who will lead you with knowledge and understanding."
– Jeremiah 3:15

"The word of the LORD came to me: 'Son of man, prophesy against the shepherds of Israel; prophesy and say to them: "This is what the Sovereign LORD says: Woe to you shepherds of Israel who only take care of yourselves! Should not shepherds take care of the flock? You eat the curds, clothe yourselves with the wool and slaughter the choice animals, but you do not take care of the flock. You have not strengthened the weak or healed the sick or bound up the injured. You have not brought back the strays or searched for the lost. You have ruled them harshly and brutally. So they were scattered because there was no shepherd, and when they were scattered they became food for all the wild animals. My sheep wandered over all the mountains and on every high hill. They were scattered over the whole earth, and no one searched or looked for them.

"Therefore, you shepherds, hear the word of the LORD: As surely as I live, declares the Sovereign LORD, because my flock lacks a shepherd and so has been plundered and has become food for all the wild animals, and because my shepherds did not search for my flock but cared for themselves rather than for my flock, therefore, you shepherds, hear the word of the LORD: This is what the Sovereign LORD says: I am against the shepherds and will hold them accountable for my flock. I will remove them from tending the flock so that the shepherds can no longer feed themselves. I will rescue my flock from their mouths, and it will no longer be food for them.

"For this is what the Sovereign LORD says: I myself will search for my sheep and look after them. As shepherds look after their scattered flocks when they are with them, so will I look after my sheep. I will rescue them from all the places where they were scattered on a day of clouds and darkness. I will bring them out from the nations and gather them from the countries, and I will bring them into their own land. I will pasture them on the mountains of Israel, in the ravines and in all the settlements in the land. I will tend them in a good pasture, and the mountain heights of Israel will be their grazing land. There they will lie down in good grazing land, and there they will feed in a rich pasture on the mountains of Israel. I myself will tend my sheep and have them lie down, declares the Sovereign LORD. I will search for the lost and bring back the strays. I will bind up the injured and strengthen the weak, but the sleek and the strong I will destroy. I will shepherd the flock with justice." ' " – Ezekiel 34:1-16

"So Christ himself gave the apostles, the prophets, the evangelists, the pastors and teachers, to equip his people for works of service, so that the body of Christ may be built up until we all reach unity in the faith and in the knowledge of the Son of God and become mature, attaining to the whole measure of the fullness of Christ. Then we will no longer be infants, tossed back and forth by the waves, and blown here and there by every wind of teaching and by the cunning and craftiness of people in their deceitful scheming. Instead,

speaking the truth in love, we will in all things grow up into him who is the head, that is, Christ. From him the whole body, joined and held together by every supporting ligament, grows and builds itself up in love, as each part does its work.
– Ephesians 4:11-16

- Examples of use today:

- Do you know anyone who has the gift of Pastor-Teacher? How can you encourage them as they exercise their spiritual gift?

- Do you believe you have the spiritual gift of Pastor-Teacher? Why?

~~DISTINGUISHING OF SPIRITS~~ prophecy

Greek: prophēteuō = speak under inspiration, speak forth the mind and counsel of God

The God-given ability, out of love for God's people, to proclaim God's truth in a way that makes it relevant to current situations in today's culture and guides others to more faith-informed decisions and actions. The goal is not to condemn, but to bring about change or enlightenment. People with this gift listen carefully to God so their words will be God-honoring. They see inconsistencies between people's words/actions and biblical teaching others overlook or may not catch. Prophets speak to the people, bringing edification, encouragement, and consolation. They warn people of the immediate or future consequences of continuing their current course of action. Sometimes we perceive that prophets bring a message of doom and gloom. In reality,

prophets speak a message of challenge for wrong direction or action, yet always end with a message of hope and restoration if the message is heeded.

Scripture References

"If I have the gift of prophecy and can fathom all mysteries and all knowledge, and if I have a faith that can move mountains, but do not have love, I am nothing."
– 1 Corinthians 13:2

"But those who prophesy speak to people for their strengthening, encouragement and comfort." – 1 Corinthians 14:3

"For you can all prophesy in turn so that everyone may be instructed or encouaged." – 1 Corinthians 14:31

"So Christ himself gave the apostles, the prophets, the evangelists, the pastors and teachers, to equip his people for works of service, so that the body of Christ may be built up until we all reach unity in the faith and in the knowledge of the Son of God and become mature, attaining to the whole measure of the fullness of Christ." – Ephesians 4:11-13

"At this I fell at his feet to worship him. But he said to me, 'Don't do that! I am a fellow servant with you and with your brothers and sisters who hold to Jesus' testimony. Worship God! For the testimony of Jesus is the Spirit of prophecy.'"
– Revelation 19:10

- Examples of use today:

- Do you know anyone who has the gift of Prophecy? How can you encourage them as they exercise their spiritual gift?

- Do you believe you have the spiritual gift of Prophecy? Why?

SPEAKING IN TONGUES

Greek: glōssa= tongues, a language, specifically one not naturally learned

The divine ability to speak a message from God to the people in a language one has not naturally learned. The gift of tongues is a sign to unbelievers showing the power and glory of God. There seem to be three types of tongues: speaking in a language the speaker does not know, but the listener does; speaking in a language neither the speaker nor the listeners understand, which requires an interpreter; and a private prayer language. The first two build up the body of Christ. The third edifies the speaker and is used in private prayer to commune with God.

Scripture References

"When the day of Pentecost came, they were all together in one place. Suddenly a sound like the blowing of a violent wind came from heaven and filled the whole house where they were sitting. They saw what seemed to be tongues of fire that separated and came to rest on each of them. All of them were filled with the Holy Spirit and began to speak in other tongues as the Spirit enabled them.

"Now there were staying in Jerusalem God-fearing Jews from every nation under heaven. When they heard this sound, a crowd came together in bewilderment, because each one heard their own language being spoken. Utterly amazed, they asked: 'Aren't all these who are speaking Galileans? Then how is it that each of us hears them in our own native language? Parthians, Medes and Elamites; residents of Mesopotamia, Judea and Cappadocia, Pontus and Asia, Phrygia and Pamphylia, Egypt and the parts of Libya near Cyrene; visitors from Rome (both Jews and converts to Judaism); Cretans and Arabs—we hear them declaring the wonders of God in our own tongues!' " – Acts 2:1-11

"If I speak in human or angelic tongues, but do not have love, I am only a resounding gong or a clanging cymbal."
– 1 Corinthians 13:1

"What then shall we say, brothers and sisters? When you come together, each of you has a hymn, or a word of instruction, a revelation, a tongue or an interpretation. Everything must be done so that the church may be built up. If anyone speaks in a tongue, two—or at the most three—should speak, one at a time, and someone must interpret. If there is no interpreter, the speaker should keep quiet in church; let them speak to themselves and to God."
– 1 Corinthians 14:26-28

"Therefore, my brothers and sisters, be eager to prophesy, and do not forbid speaking in tongues. But everything should be done in a fitting and orderly way."
– 1 Corinthians 14:39-40

- Examples of use today:

- Do you know anyone who has the gift of Speaking in Tongues? How can you encourage them as they exercise their spiritual gift?

- Do you believe you have the spiritual gift of Speaking in Tongues? Why?

proclaiming God's truth

TEACHING

Greek: didaskalia = instruction, the act of imparting the truth

The divine ability to understand and clearly explain God's truths, and to show how we can apply these in our lives. People with this gift enjoy studying the Bible and inspire listeners to greater obedience to God's word. They prepare through study and reflection and pay close attention to detail. In addition to communicating facts, they are careful to show that the Scriptures have practical applications. They can adapt their presentation in order to communicate God's message to a particular audience effectively.

Scripture References

"Therefore go and make disciples of all nations, baptizing them in the name of the Father and of the Son and of the Holy Spirit, and teaching them to obey everything I have commanded you."
– Matthew 28:19-20a

"We proclaim him, admonishing and teaching everyone with all wisdom, so that we present everyone fully mature in Christ." – Colossians 1:28

"Not many of you should presume to be teachers, my brothers and sisters, because you know that we who teach will be judged more strictly." – James 3:1

"And of this gospel I was appointed a herald and an apostle and a teacher."
– 2 Timothy 1:11

- Examples of use today:

- Do you know anyone who has the gift of Teaching? How can you encourage them as they exercise their spiritual gift?

- Do you believe you have the spiritual gift of Teaching? Why?

instruction

MESSAGE OF WISDOM

Greek: logos = something said, utterance, communication
sophia= wisdom, higher or lower, earthly or spiritual

The God-given ability to understand and apply biblical and spiritual knowledge to complex, contradictory, or other difficult situations. People with the gift of Message of Wisdom have an ability to understand and live God's will. They share their wisdom with others through teaching and admonition. As with the gift of Message of Knowledge, the term "message of wisdom" is intentional. The wisdom is not for one's own benefit, but must be shared. People with this gift speak God's truth as found in Scripture, in order to provide clarity and direction to people who are struggling with which way they should go. They make practical application of biblical truths. They are, in effect, a "compass" for the body of Christ.

Scripture References

"For this reason, since the day we heard about you, we have not stopped praying for you. We continually ask God to fill you with the knowledge of his will through all the wisdom and understanding that the Spirit gives, so that you may live a life worthy of the Lord and please him in every way; bearing fruit in every good work, growing in the knowledge of God, being strengthened with all power according to his glorious might so that you may have great endurance and patience, and giving joyful thanks to the Father, who has qualified you to share in the inheritance of his people in the kingdom of light."
– Colossians 1:9-12

"We proclaim him, admonishing and teaching everyone with all wisdom, so that we may present everyone fully mature in Christ." – Colossians 1:28

"Let the message of Christ dwell among you richly as you teach and admonish one another with all wisdom through psalms, hymns and songs from the Spirit, singing to God with gratitude in your hearts." – Colossians 3:16

"Who is wise and understanding among you? Let them show it by their good life, by deeds in the humility that comes from wisdom. But if you harbor bitter envy and selfish ambition in your hearts, do not boast about it or deny the truth. Such 'wisdom' does not come down from heaven but is earthly, unspiritual, demonic. For where you have envy and selfish ambition, there you find disorder and every evil practice.

"But the wisdom that comes from heaven is first of all pure; then peace-oving, considerate, submissive, full of mercy and good fruit, impartial and sincere." – James 3:13-17

- Examples of use today:

- Do you know anyone who has the gift of Message of Wisdom? How can you encourage them as they exercise their spiritual gift?

- Do you believe you have the spiritual gift of Message of Wisdom? Why?

THINKING ABOUT YOUR GIFTS

As we mentioned earlier, many books have been written about spiritual gifts. They can be contradictory and confusing. Make sure you judge the validity of what they say against the Bible. After all, God's word is our "plumb line."

Review your scores from the Spiritual Gifts Discovery Tool (pages 23-29). List the three gifts for which you scored the highest numbers in the blanks provided on these pages. Reread the Bible passages listed in this chapter for those gifts, and write down notes and reflections that you find significant.

1. _____
   _____
   _____

2. _____
   _____
   _____

3. _____
   _____
   _____

Let's close this leg of your journey by contemplating the benefits of discovering, developing, and using your spiritual gifts.

Church Benefits

• Churches that teach and develop gifts-based ministries are more effective in the ministries they provide. Churches with gifts-based ministries have people with the gift of Leadership leading, people with the gift of Helps and people with the gift of Mercy reaching out to persons who are suffering, and so on.

• Churches that teach and develop gifts-based ministries grow spiritually. When God's people use their gifts in service to others, they see God at work, changing lives and changing the world—one person at a time.

Personal Benefits

• You will have a better understanding of God's purpose for your life. God gives each person unique gifts to fulfill God's specific plan.

• Your relationship with God will grow and mature. As you minister to others and see the difference God makes in their lives through you, your relationship with God will deepen.

• Your ministry will be more joy-filled and effective. For example, if you have a passion for children and the gift of teaching, you will probably be a very effective children's Sunday school teacher. Doing it will energize you!

<h3 style="text-align:center">Notes/Reflections/Questions about Spiritual Gifts</h3>

"When God's people use their gifts in service to others, they see God at work."

Talents & Resources

CHAPTER 3

Talents and Resources

Therefore, I urge you, brothers and sisters, in view of God's mercy, to offer your bodies as a living sacrifice, holy and pleasing to God—this is true worship.—Romans 12:1

You did not choose me, but I chose you and appointed you so that you might go and bear fruit—fruit that will last— and so that whatever you ask in my name the Father will give you.—John 15:16

Talents

The "T" in S.T.R.I.D.E. stands for our Talents—both God-given and acquired. Every person is born with natural talents, whether for athletics, music, arithmetic, mechanics, or something else altogether. Talents are those abilities that seem to "come naturally." See if you can identify the talents of the following people:

Peyton Manning   _____

Celine Dion   _____

Bill Gates   _____

John Grisham   _____

Sometimes we confuse talents with spiritual gifts. They can seem very similar, because both refer to an exceptional ability to do something. Natural abilities may mirror gifts, but there are some differences. Spiritual gifts are given to Christians, while every person (Christian or not) is born with natural talents. Talents are sometimes used to benefit others, but they can also be used for self-edification. Spiritual gifts are only used to glorify God and to serve others.

One way to distinguish whether an ability is a talent or a spiritual gift is to consider the purpose and the results. Does the ability serve others and glorify God? Spiritual gifts will have a "yes" answer to both parts of this question.

Acquired skills and expertise can be used to serve others and glorify God as well. Public speaking, facilitation skills, writing, and expertise in computers, graphic arts, or audiovideo technology can all have a place serving within the body of Christ.

Sometimes people use their natural talents or acquired skills in concert with their spiritual gifts. For examples, Oleta Adams, a wonderful blues singer from Kansas City, has a tremendous musical talent. She was raised as a child in the church (her father is a pastor), but she didn't have a personal faith in Christ. As an adult she sang in bars and clubs. When she came into a personal relationship with Christ, God gave her the spiritual gift of Encouragement. She now uses her natural musical talent with her spiritual gift of Encouragement by singing songs that glorify God. Her message strengthens and encourages others to follow Christ.

God can also transform our natural talents into spiritual gifts. For instance, God may elevate and amplify someone's natural leadership to the point of a spiritual gift when he or she enters into a believing relationship with Jesus Christ.

Some jobs or tasks cannot be completed without help from God. We have to be open to letting God work through us for great things to happen. In the Bible, when the Moabites and Ammonites came to make war against King Jehoshaphat and the Israelites in 2 Chronicles 20, Jehoshaphat called upon the Lord for help. The Lord answered him saying, "Do not be afraid or discouraged because of this vast army. For the battle is not yours, but God's" (2 Chronicles 20:15). The same is true for us today as we serve God. We need to "get out of the way" and let the Holy Spirit work through us. We are only the instruments.

When Yvonne first agreed to teach Spiritual Gifts Discovery, she based her decision on the fact that she had experience speaking in front of groups, and she had studied the material. She thought that she could handle it on the merit of her own abilities. The first two classes did not go well. Finally, one evening after class, she went home in tears. She prayed to God, "Maybe I'm in the wrong place again! I can't do this! I need your help. Next week, I'll show up, but you'll have to teach the class. If you don't want me doing this, I'll know."

Amazingly, the next week it was as if the Holy Spirit DID teach the class. Yvonne's speaking ability was used, but the difference was that now she was willing to allow the Holy Spirit to work through her, instead of relying on her own abilities.

What are your natural talents or acquired skills that God could use for God's purposes?

One note: using your spiritual gifts and/or your talents to serve God is meant to bring you joy and fulfillment. We have spoken with people who have expressed thoughts like, "I know I am a gifted (highly skilled) teacher, because that's what I do for a living and I have earned recognition for that. However, the thought of doing that on the weekends, too, just DEPRESSES me!" You might call these "killer talents." They are things we are really good at, but sometimes too much of a good thing can cause stress/fatigue/failure. If you're trying to figure out whether using one of your known gifts or abilities is God's will for your ministry, one gauge is to determine whether doing so would bring you pleasure or whether it would drain your batteries. Remember— service is meant to bring YOU joy, too.

We need to recognize that all abilities come from God. In that sense, they are gifts and can be dedicated to God's use. What makes spiritual gifts distinct is that God owns the results. God gets the credit, because what is accomplished is beyond our own abilities. In the Bible passage that opens this chapter, Paul's instruction is to "offer your bodies as a living sacrifice." That means our whole selves—our gifts, our talents, our dreams, our individuality, and our resources, which we'll cover next.

Notes/Reflections on Talents

"What makes spiritual gifts distinct is that God owns the results."

Resources

When we think of resources, most of us usually think of financial resources. These are certainly a part of our resource pool, but there is so much more. Our resources include our finances, our time, our material possessions, our contacts, our hobbies, and many other items. The question we ask in this chapter is, "How do we best utilize the resources God has given us to have an impact for God's purposes?"

There is an old saying that goes something like this: "I've never seen a hearse towing a U-Haul® trailer behind it." The meaning is pretty clear—you can't take it with you. However, this saying leaves out an important teaching of Christ—you can't take it with you, but you can send it on ahead. In Matthew 6:19-21, Christ says these words:

"Do not store up for yourselves treasures on earth, where moth and rust destroy, and where thieves break in and steal. But store up for yourselves treasures in heaven, where moth and rust do not destroy, and where thieves do not break in and steal. For where your treasure is, there your heart will be also."

Christ instructed us here to invest in things that have eternal value. Only two things are eternal: God and people. How do we invest in these? By being good stewards of our resources.

Jesus used a great parable to explain the stewardship of our resources. In the Today's New International Version of the Bible it is often called the parable of the Bags of Gold, but in other translations, it is called the Parable of the Talents (talents were a type of currency in Jesus' time).

The Parable of the Bags of Gold

"Again, it will be like a man going on a journey, who called his servants and entrusted his wealth to them. To one he gave five bags of gold, to another two bags, and to another one bag, each according to his ability. Then he went on his journey. The man who had received five bags of gold went at once and put his money to work and gained five bags more. So also, the one with two bags of gold gained two more. But the man who had received one bag went off, dug a hole in the ground and hid his master's money.

"After a long time the master of those servants returned and settled accounts with them. The man who had received five bags of gold brought the other five. 'Master,' he said, 'you entrusted me with five bags of gold. See, I have gained five more.'

"His master replied, 'Well done, good and faithful servant! You have been faithful with a few things; I will put you in charge of many things. Come and share your master's happiness!'

"The man with two bags of gold also came. 'Master,' he said, 'you entrusted me with two bags of gold; see, I have gained two more.'

"His master replied, 'Well done, good and faithful servant! You have been faithful with a few things; I will put you in charge of many things. Come and share your master's happiness!'

"Then the man who had received one bag of gold came. 'Master' he said, 'I knew that you are a hard man, harvesting where you have not sown and gathering where you have not scattered seed. So I was afraid and went out and hid your gold in the ground. See, here is what belongs to you.'

"His master replied, 'You wicked, lazy servant! So you knew that I harvest where I have not sown and gather where I have not scattered seed? Well then, you should have put my money on deposit with the bankers, so that when I returned I would have received it back with interest.

'Take the bag of gold from him and give it to the one who has ten bags. For those who have will be given more, and they will have an abundance. As for those who do not have, even what they have will be taken from them. And throw that worthless servant outside, into the darkness, where there will be weeping and gnashing of teeth.' " – Matthew 25:14-30

good stewards

Have you ever heard the saying, "From those to whom much is given, much will be expected"? This is the message of this parable. We all receive much from God. All that we have is from God. What we have is not ours to keep for ourselves—or to hide in a hole in the ground—but is ours to use while we are here on earth. We are only stewards of all that we have. How can you put your resources to use for God?

Investing in things that are eternal also includes setting priorities based on our values and then living by those priorities. The story of Mary and Martha is an example of this. You may remember the story. Jesus was visiting their house . . .

"As Jesus and his disciples were on their way, he came to a village where a woman named Martha opened her home to him. She had a sister called Mary, who sat at the Lord's feet listening to what he said. But Martha was distracted by all the preparations that had to be made. She came to him and asked, 'Lord, don't you care that my sister has left me to do the work by myself? Tell her to help me!'

'Martha, Martha,' the Lord answered, 'you are worried and upset about many things, but few things are needed—or indeed only one. Mary has chosen what is better, and it will not be taken away from her.'" – Luke 10:38-42

We can use our material resources in many ways to glorify God. One member of our church has a small farm with animals. She volunteers the use of her donkey and lamb for our Christmas pageant every year. Another member opens her home to members of the church for fellowship activities. Yet another member bakes fabulous bread for various events.

Our contacts (the people in our address books) are resources, too. Perhaps we can ask them to speak to our Sunday school class or other group. Maybe they can help with a project or be a resource for ideas or information.

All of these things—the things we own or have access to—can be used by God. The most important resource for us to consider, though, when trying to find a place of service within the body of Christ, is our time. When you are weighing different service opportunities, you should carefully consider the time commitment that is expected in light of the time you have available to give. Depending on your circumstances or stage of life, you may have an hour a month to serve or five hours a day.

Various service opportunities, likewise, are going to require different time commitments. Objectively considering the time commitment required for each service opportunity and your ability to meet that expectation will help you either eliminate some opportunities as not good matches for you (at least not at this time), or might help you build your list of "potential good matches" for further consideration or exploration.

Finding an opportunity that is a "good match" is a critical component of making a successful service connection—both for you and the ministry that is served. It benefits no one for you to sign up for a particular position and then be unable to fulfill the obligation. Better to put them on the "maybe later" list if you think it's something you're still interested in pursuing.

- What are your resources?

- How can you use them to serve others and to glorify God?

Notes/Reflections on Resources

consider the time commitment

Individuality

CHAPTER 4

Individuality

There is one body and one Spirit, just as you were called to
one hope when you were called; one Lord, one faith, one
baptism; one God and Father of all, who is over all and
through all and in all. But to each one of us grace has been
given as Christ apportioned it.
– Ephesians 4:4-7

Just as, by God's design, no two snowflakes are exactly alike, God created people to be unique individuals. No one in all of God's creation is exactly like you. That is amazing even to think about. You are a genuine, one-copy original, with a style all your own.

Determining our "Individuality" is important as we consider the ways in which we will serve God. Our style affects the way we think, expend and receive our energy, organize our work, and interact with other people. Many instruments are available today to help people determine their style or personality type. Perhaps you have taken one through your employer, community group, or church.

For simplicity's sake, we will focus on two key components of style that most directly impact service: (1) energy focus and (2) preferred environment. In our discussion of energy focus, we'll talk about extroverts and introverts. When we shift to preferred environment, we'll focus on whether you prefer a flexible or a stable environment.

Can we determine a person's style just by watching them? Not necessarily. For instance, Emily speaks quite well in front of groups and seems to make small talk with ease. She introduces herself to new people and makes them feel welcome to the group. She always has a smile on her face and is usually the first one to tell a joke. What do you think: extrovert or introvert? Actually, Emily is an extreme introvert, but her career as a business owner requires her to operate outside of her instinctive style. She took a course in public speaking and human relations to help her get out of her "comfort zone." Now she does those things with seeming effortlessness, but they are still not "comfortable" to her. They are not natural actions, but learned behaviors.

As you go through this chapter, try to focus on what is "natural" for you—what is instinctive—not what you have learned to do or what is required of you in your career, family, or other environment.

Energy Focus

Depending on how you are "wired," you are either considered an introvert or an extrovert. Since 1921, when psychiatrist Carl Jung (1875-1961) wrote *Psychological Types*, scholars and scientists have been exploring personality differences. Jung wrote about the now famous types, "introverts" and "extroverts," examining how individuals take in the world, renew their energy and, through other type distinctions, how they process information, schedule their time, and express their feelings. People sometimes misunderstand the dynamics of these words, believing that extroverts are boisterous, gregarious, outgoing individuals, while introverts are quiet, reserved, and humble. While this may be the case in some instances, these views are stereotypes. The terms *introvert* and *extrovert* have more to do with the ways in which we receive and expend energy—or our energy focus—than how verbal we may or may not be.

Another way to look at personality types, building on this work, can be found in David Keirsey's work. He suggests that some people gain energy, like being powered by batteries, from other people. Long periods of quiet and individual work are exhausting for them. Others draw energy from solitary activities, working alone on a project that captures their passion whether it is simple or difficult. These individuals become exhausted in large groups or from extended contact with others.

Someone whose style leans more heavily toward the introverted side of the continuum will be energized more through times of quiet reflection and accomplishment of goals than by interaction with people. Extroverts will often find themselves drained of energy when they are deprived of people-interaction or bogged down with a project. Of course, these examples represent extremes. Most people find themselves somewhere between the two. Where they find themselves may also very well depend upon their circumstances.

Why is it important to understand your style when you are considering where to serve? Well, let's think about that for minute. . . . If you prefer to interact with a lot of people, and you volunteer to serve in an area where you are performing behind-the-scenes functions with little opportunity to be with other people, how might that make you feel? Restless? Bored? Closed off? On the other hand, if you like to work quietly to accomplish goals, interacting with people on occasion, how would you feel if the position in which you serve puts you in a large group of people with little time for working on projects and gives you no quiet time to yourself? Frustrated? Uncomfortable?

You may immediately know whether your Individuality is more extroverted or introverted. Just in case you don't, here are a few questions that may help you determine your style.

Try to answer using the word that best describes what you prefer, not what your current work, church, or home circumstances dictate. Circle the word or phrase that best matches how you would complete each statement, and make notes or comments in the space allowed. A few questions are included after each statement for you to think about as you consider a potential ministry position.

I usually: enjoy center stage or shun the limelight.

Think about this in a ministry setting. If the position requires you to be the focus of attention often, will it energize you or will it make you uncomfortable?

People who meet me would describe me as: easy to get to know or quiet and reserved.

As you consider a ministry position, will you be asked to meet new people often? How would you like that? Or will you develop relationships with a more stable group of people? Which is more to your liking?

I develop ideas through: discussion or internal thought.

Will you be required to share your thoughts and feelings in a group setting? Or will you be asked to develop ideas and then present them? Which do you prefer?

When my work is interrupted, I: welcome the diversion or get impatient with the distraction.

As you think about a particular ministry position, will there be many interruptions as you go about the task? Will you enjoy that? Or will that be a bother to you?

introvert or extrovert?

I work best: in a group or independently.

Some people really enjoy working with a group, while others enjoy more solitary pursuits. Which is your preference? When you consider stepping into a ministry position, consider whether it is a good fit with this preference.

I prefer to communicate with people via: telephone or e-mail.

Some ministry positions have a lot of personal communication with others, while some positions involve a lot of e-mail communication in between a small amount of personal contact. Which is more your style?

When my "batteries" need recharging, I: go out with friends or spend some quiet time alone.

This question is important as you consider a place of service. Will the position allow you to get your batteries recharged according to your preference? Make sure the position you serve in is not one that only "drains your batteries" without permitting you time and opportunity for "recharging."

How did you answer these questions? If you circled the first choice in each of the statements, you are more likely to be an extrovert. If more of the second answers fit, you are more likely to be an introvert. Are you more extroverted or introverted? Still can't decide? In meetings, do you tend to "think out loud"? Or do you usually consider your thoughts and ideas carefully before sharing them? Think about what you do when you are tired or stressed out. Do you get together with friends to "forget about it" or "get recharged"? Or are you more likely to need time alone to just "chill"? Do you find it easy to talk with just about anyone you meet? Or is it easier for you to talk with people you have known for a while? Consider your instinctive responses, not what you have learned to do.

Remember that most of us fit somewhere in between the two extremes and, in fact, operate all along the continuum, moving back and forth during our day. Usually, though, we are more comfortable and would prefer to operate in one place most of the time. When we serve in an area that is opposite of our preference, we can do it; but after a while, doing so will drain us of our energy, instead of making us feel energized.

Take a look at the continuum below and think about where you fit. Make a mark there:

|_____|_____|

Extrovert	Middle	Introvert
(energized through interaction)		(energized through reflection)

Finding yourself near the middle of the continuum may simply mean that situations in which you find yourself will dictate your preferred response.

Remember: Extroverts also accomplish tasks and introverts also love people. The purpose of this exercise is to determine which of the two scenarios recharge your batteries and revive your spirit. When it comes to serving God in the church or out in the community, you will want to find yourself in a place of service where you are energized rather than where you are constantly drained of energy.

Preferred Environment

The term *preferred environment* describes how you prefer to work in any setting. This means what you do in the context of your job, at home, in the church, or anyplace where you do anything. In order to accomplish the task at hand, people tend to prefer either a stable environment or a flexible one.

Generally speaking, a person who prefers a stable environment likes to work within the realm of deadlines, structure, accountability, and systems. He or she will find systems freeing and comfortable, because then they know exactly what to expect and what is expected of them. Individuals who prefer a flexible environment find structure, deadlines, and systems to be confining. The "flexible" person prefers to focus on the end product, leaving the details of how to get there subject to change and interpretation.

Let's talk about why this might be important. If you prefer flexibility in your environment, and you serve in an area that requires you to follow specific steps to accomplish your goals with no room for "interpretation," how will you feel? Stifled? Bored? Or if you prefer a stable environment, and you serve in an area where things are always changing, where you never do the same thing twice or the same thing twice the same way, how will that make you feel? Uncomfortable? Insecure?

Once again, you may be able to identify immediately your own preferred environment. Just in case you can't, the following exercise is designed to help you make a determination about where you might fit on the continuum. Keep in mind, as you did with the previous exercise, to answer the questions based upon your own preference, not on the situations in which you currently find yourself at work, at home, in your community, or at church. Make any notes or comments in the space provided.

When I'm working on a project, I like to: adapt as I go or plan ahead.

When you are considering a place of service, think about the structure that may be required. If you "plan your work and then work your plan," but the position requires a great deal of flexibility and many last-minute changes, will you feel stressed?

I tend to work with: spurts of energy at the last minute or regular, steady effort.

If you work in bursts of energy, will the position allow you that freedom, or will it require meeting deadlines all along the way? On the other hand, if you like regular, steady effort, will there be enough structure and focus to keep you happy?

When I plan my activities, the plans are: "penciled in" or final.

Do you like to "keep your options open" or do you prefer to make decisions and move on? Think about how you plan your vacation. Do you make a general plan for activities that is open to change, or do you make reservations for every activity? Determine whether the ministry position

you are considering will be a good "fit" for you in this regard.

I like: spontaneity or predictability.

Do you feel more comfortable when you know what to expect? Or do you get bored with routine? Think about how this might apply to a ministry setting. If the position is the same every day, will you be relaxed and confident, or will you be bored silly?

I tend to: have more than one project going on at once or finish one thing before going on to the next.

Think about your typical "to do" list. Do you check everything off, or do you often get most things completed and leave others for another day? Will the position require multitasking, or will it require a step-by-step process, one project at a time? Which is more to your liking?

I prefer decisions that: are open to discussion or provide closure.

When you make decisions, or hear a decision that someone else has made, think about your response. Do you change your mind often (if you made the decision), or do you still listen to input from others? If someone else makes the decision, do you get annoyed if they later change their decision, or do you admire their flexibility? How might this apply in a ministry setting?

I usually dress for: comfort or appearance.

Think about your "style." Do you like to dress casually, more for comfort and convenience than for style? Or do you prefer to look neat and "polished." Consider this in broader terms than dress. Are you more of a serious person or a more light-hearted person? Do you like to be in control, or do you like to "wait and see"? Will the ministry position be a good fit in this regard?

How did you answer the questions? Do you prefer a stable or a more flexible environment? If you were more likely to choose the first response in each pair, you are more likely to prefer a flexible environment. If the second responses seem to fit more often, you may find a stable environment more appealing. Can't decide? Think about a project you have worked on. Did you form a general plan, but then adapt and change course when you thought it was appropriate? Or did you plan everything in detail and then follow that plan? Do you mix work and play? Or do you follow the mantra, work before play? Do you get excited when you start a project? Or do you get more pleasure out of finishing a project? Take a look at the continuum and think about where you fit. Place a mark there:

|_____|_____|

Flexible   **Middle**   **Stable**
Adapt as I go   Plan ahead

Hopefully, answering these questions has aided you in determining your preferred environment. In some instances, both word choices might fit you. However, you will still likely have a preference for one over the other, slight though it may be. For example, the flexible person might love multiple options when working on a project, but still long for closure at some point.

If you do not fall neatly into one category or the other, take heart. Try to give thought to the very best environment you can imagine and prepare yourself to articulate your needs for a service setting. You will find less frustration when you can clearly choose a place to serve God that is in harmony with the unique way in which God has created you.

Putting It All Together

On the space below, write out the combination of energy focus and preferred environment that best describes you (extrovert/stable; extrovert/flexible; introvert/stable; introvert/flexible):

I am

_____.

Now it's time to take the next step and consider what these style combinations mean when it comes to serving God. Remember at the start of this chapter when you read about the implications of style? Our Individuality affects the way we think, receive and expend our energy, organize our work, and interact with other people. Let's connect these concepts to serving God in the church and community for each of the four style combinations. While we are suggesting some areas where each of these types might work or serve, remember that many other things need to be considered: your spiritual gifts, what you are passionate about, your talents and acquired skills, and so forth. So don't be discouraged if the suggestions are not right for you. As we said in the beginning, you are unique!

Extrovert/Stable

If you are an extrovert/stable individual, then you may be energized by interaction with people, but you will likely prefer to interact with people in predetermined settings and at scheduled times. You value effectiveness and efficiency, tend to be practical, yet are outgoing and warm.

Communication with this type of person should be personal, goals need to be specific, and any service must be relevant to the needs of another.

Preferred careers for those with this style combination may be counselors, social workers, child-care providers, small business owners, health-care workers, and receptionists. In the church—based solely upon style—you may be drawn to people-oriented service opportunities such as pastoral care ministry, small group leadership, greeter, usher, hospitality provider, recognition team member, intercessory prayer, nursery or preschool, or a mission ministry with direct but predictable people contact.

A word of caution: this type tends to overcommit to work and overinvest emotionally.

Extrovert/Flexible

If you are an extrovert/flexible individual, you are energized by people-interaction. You enjoy more spontaneity and less structure, more fun and less practicality. You value creativity, exude enthusiasm, welcome change, and have the capacity to be engaging and inspirational. Communication with this type of person should be direct and frequent, goals need to be "big picture," and the best service opportunity will capitalize on the ability to market and promote the ministry.

Preferred careers for the extrovert/flexible person might be marketing personnel, politicians, actors, consultants, teachers, and sales agents. Within the church, this type of person might be well-suited for a ministry opportunity involving team-building, event planning, youth group leading, teaching Bible classes and workshops, drama team directing, or marketing new programs.

A word of caution: this type may lose sight of important details or have trouble keeping enough focus to accomplish the goal.

Introvert/Stable

If you are an introvert/stable individual, you tend to be quiet, reflective, and practical. You learn through research and observation. You value consistency and preservation. In your opinion, systems, policies, and procedures were designed to be followed to the letter.

Communication with this type of person should be direct and detailed, goals need to be practical, and service in the church must be organized and reliable.

Preferred careers might include accountants, school principals, carpenters, clerical supervisors, clergy, military officers, and technicians in various fields. If you are this type of person, every ministry area will desire you to help organize the necessary details and weigh all the options. You might be drawn to serve in the financial or facilities ministries of the church, help with the office work—including collating bulletins or data entry or mailings—edit publications, or help with audiovisual and computer technology ministries.

A word of caution: this type can exhibit nitpicking tendencies, become bogged down with details, or lose sight of the "big picture."

Introvert/Flexible

If you are an introvert/flexible individual, you tend to be direct, visionary, focused, confident, and competitive. You value results, big dreams, thorough research, and independent thinking.

Communication with this type of person should be direct and concise, goals should be visionary, and a service position in the church must include versatility, general guidelines, and reasonable authority.

If you are this type of person, you may

be drawn to a career as a lawyer, architect, senior pastor, manager or executive, engineer, journalist, or physician. In the church, you might consider leading a team or committee, organizing an event or campaign, teaching Sunday school, leading a mission trip, or serving as a group facilitator.

A word of caution: this type may be perceived as pushy, controlling, or arrogant, and would do well to remember that the thoughts, ideas, and contributions of others are valuable and necessary.

Conclusion

Every ministry area and team within the church benefits from having each of the four style combinations represented. A ministry or program stands a better chance of succeeding with each of these styles in balance. Goals will be set and met, people inspired and challenged, details organized efficiently, and everyone's efforts encouraged and celebrated. God will be glorified!

When it comes to dealing with people, they will not always fit neatly on a grid or continuum. We have to let go of linear thinking and remember that human beings are much more complex and diverse. They cannot be pigeonholed into a category. Yet knowing our Individuality—and the styles of those with whom we interact—can provide important clues to help us communicate more effectively, avoid conflict, articulate our service environment needs, and serve with less frustration and more joy. That is precisely what God wants for us . . . a place to serve and glorify God where we can be our best selves, fulfilling God's perfect design!

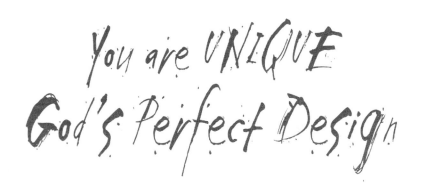

Notes/Reflections on Individuality

What is your combination?

Dreams

"God places a dream...in each of our hearts."

CHAPTER 5

Dreams

Hope deferred makes the heart sick,
but a longing fulfilled is a tree of life.
—Proverbs 13:12

In his book, *The Call*, Os Guinness writes, *"The truth is not that God is finding us a place for our gifts but that God has created us and our gifts for a place of his choosing—and we will only be ourselves when we are finally there"* (Nashville: Word Publishing Group, 2003, 1998; p. 47). Wayne Cordeiro, pastor of New Hope Christian Fellowship in Hawaii, put it this way, *"If God's whole purpose in saving you was to have you baptized and get you into heaven, He would have had you shot as you left your baptism! The fact that He left you here means He has plans for you—there is something He wants you to accomplish"* (Public Speech. New Century, New Church Conference. San Antonio, Tx 1998). God cares about every need that exists on earth. God does not want anyone to be hurting, or sick, or alone, or lost. God counts on us to be God's hands and voice in this broken world; but God knows that we, as individuals, can't possibly care about every need. For that reason, much like a parent dividing household chores among children, God places a dream (a desire, a passion, a calling) in each of our hearts.

In his book, *Doing Church as a Team*, Wayne Cordeiro writes, *"In every person's heart is a dream of what he or she can become for the Lord; a dream that sees them making a difference in the world, in their families, and in their churches"* (Regal Books, 2004; p. 111). Unlike household chores, though, God makes us passionate about the calling God has for us. Because we are passionate about it, we are happy and successful when we are serving in that area. If each us understands the dream that God has given us, and fulfills that calling, the body of Christ can meet every need, heal every hurt, and save every lost lamb.

Where is it that you would like to make a difference? For a few people, this may seem simple. Most people struggle with it, however. We have heard many people say things like, "I'm not really passionate about anything!" One thing is for sure: Most of us have a clear understanding of what we don't want to do! Since we will not feel fulfilled until we're serving in an area about which we are passionate, we have a real need to discover our dreams. Guinness writes, "In many cases, a clear sense of calling comes only through a time of searching, including trial and error" (p. 52). If you have never been exposed to the area in which God wants you to serve, you will probably not recognize it until you do try it out.

"Trial and error" can be intimidating. It means taking risks and just trying something new! When you think about it, what makes it worthwhile to take such risks? Such risks are worthwhile because they make us utterly dependent upon God, not on ourselves. When we try serving in a new area, we are blazing a new trail in our life. In his song by the same title, Steven Curtis Chapman compares the Christian life to *"The Great Adventure"*—and says that this journey of faith requires us to follow our Leader into *"the glorious unknown"* (Sparrow Records, 1992). Having the faith to risk stepping out of our comfort zone stretches us, and makes the Great Adventure more real.

The body of Christ should be an environment where we are free to take such risks—free to fail with a group of supporters to pick us up, brush us off, and put us back in the saddle again (or maybe in a different saddle!).

> If I'm not free to fail, I'm not free to take risks, and everything in life that's worth doing involves a willingness to take a risk and involves a risk of failure. . . . I have to try, but I do not have to succeed. Following Christ has nothing to do with success as the world sees success.
> —Madeleine L'Engle (as quoted in *Secret Longings of the Heart,* by Carol Kent (NavPress, 2003; p. 147)

Sometimes we are afraid because we are being called into an area that seems beyond our capabilities or experience. Thankfully, it's not our own capabilities or experience on which we have to rely, but on the power of the Holy Spirit. We look through a peephole, while God encourages us to open the door and see the whole panorama.

In his book, *What You Do Best in the Body of Christ*, Bruce Bugbee lists three types of dreams that seem to pop up again and again: *dreams of making a difference for individual persons or groups of people; dreams of making a difference in connection with some worthwhile cause; and dreams of making a difference through some role or function* (Zondervan, 1995; pp. 35-36). For example, some persons may dream of helping specific groups of people, such as elderly persons, or youth, or single parents. Others may dream of conquering AIDS, or hunger, or homelessness. Still others may dream of making a difference through mentoring, or promoting stewardship, or using skills or specific gifts. Don't limit your dreams to these categories, though; they may fall outside of them.

Yvonne's husband, Frank, has always been nuts about gadgets. If it has buttons, switches, lights, or wires, he loves it! He volunteered to help out by handling the audio equipment during Saturday night worship. A year later, he was on staff part-time, handling all of the audio needs of the Church of the Resurrection. This work allowed him to serve the Lord while doing something about which he's passionate. Several years later, this ministry grew into a full-time position as Worship Unit Director, overseeing all aspects of video, lighting, and set production for worship. Frank views this not as a job though, but as a full-time ministry that enables him to use his gifts and his passion to further God's kingdom.

Discovering your dream and then actually fulfilling it can change your life. Have you ever known someone who believed that serving God was supposed to be drudgery? A cross to be carried? We do not believe that is God's intention. God wants God's children to be filled with joy. Serving in an area about which you are passionate is a blessing. It provides a compass, giving you direction about where to serve; fueling motivation and energy, helping you avoid burnout; providing joy and fulfillment, as you watch your dreams become reality.

Those who hope in the LORD
will renew their strength.
They will soar on wings like eagles;
they will run and not grow weary,
they will walk and not be faint.
—Isaiah 40:31

What makes life worthwhile is having a big enough objective, something which catches our imagination and lays hold of our allegiance, and this the Christian has, in a way that no other man has. For what higher, more exalted, and more compelling goal can there be than to know God?
— J. I. Packer (as quoted in *Secret Longings of the Heart*, by Carol Kent. Knowing God (InterVarsity, 2004; p. 46)

Let's take time now to answer a few questions that may point you in the direction of your dreams. These questions are taken from the books *Healing the Purpose of Your Heart* by Dennis, Sheila, and

Matthew Linn, and from *The Path* by Laurie Beth Jones.

What are your interests? What do you like to do in your spare time? What topics draw and keep your attention?

What world/cultural events, trends, movements, or issues get you excited?

What world/cultural events, trends, movements, or issues make you angry or frustrated?

What would you do if you had the time and money to do anything?

What do you enjoy doing so much that time seems to fly when you're doing it?

Ask your friends and family for their opinions about where your passions/interests lie. The observations of others can be very telling. What insights did they have?

What are you most grateful for today? For what are you least grateful? If you were to ask yourself these questions every day, what pattern would you see?

When have you felt most alive? What are the times of your life you would most like to repeat?

If you could do anything with no chance of failure, what would you do?

Is there something that you have to do—that you can't not do?

If you had only one year to live, what would you do?

Look for patterns in your answers. Are there issues or topics that keep coming up? Don't forget to ask others what they think. Others can often see passions in you that you don't recognize. Sometimes we're too close to circumstances to see patterns. As the old saying goes, "You can't see the forest for the trees."

Try using the process of elimination to discover where you dream about making a difference. Sometimes it's easier to decide what you don't want to do, so use that as a place to start. For instance, Yvonne knows that she does not really enjoy working with elementary-age children, so she eliminated that age group from her choices. She isn't particularly passionate about ministering to homeless people, either. She is compassionate toward them, but not passionate. In the end, by eliminating some groups or activities, she was able to focus on what she did want to do and to which group she wanted to minister—adults seeking to find how God had designed them for ministry or leadership.

Is there a particular age group of people with which you enjoy spending time? Is there a particular age group you would prefer NOT to work with?

What groups of people touch your heart (such as older adults, persons who are homeless, people going through divorces)? Are there specific groups of people with whom you are NOT drawn to work?

Are there activities you really enjoy and would like to incorporate into ministry (such as gardening, music, sports, and so forth)?

Look over your top three spiritual gifts. Is there one that you would enjoy using regardless of the situation or setting? Is there a skill or talent that you want to put to use somewhere, but don't have a specific ministry area in mind?

Have you noticed a need somewhere that you feel compelled to address?

Is there a ministry you were involved with in the past that you really enjoyed? What is it? Is there one in which you were not so effective or fulfilled, and so have no further desire to explore? What about these experiences made them good, or not so good, for you?

Finding your dream is more of a journey than an event. It often requires trying a few things out to see if you like them. It should be a prayerful process. Ask for God's guidance. It can take a while. But once you discover your dreams, you cannot help but work to see them realized. They are like an emotional magnet drawing you in.

His word is in my heart like a fire,
a fire shut up in my bones.
I am weary of holding it in;
indeed, I cannot.
—Jeremiah 20:9

This calls for a word of caution: Because recognizing our dreams involves our feelings and emotions, we need to be sure our dreams are in harmony with God's will. Our dreams and goals should never contradict God's word in the Bible.

Another thing to note regarding dreams: We have been asked many times, "Well, if this is God's dream for my life, should I quit my job and do this full time?" As was the case with Yvonne's husband, it does happen on occasion. But most of the time, a person's work supports or subsidizes the dream, not replaces it. Yvonne's full-time job is still in the corporate world, while teaching and writing fulfill something internal her "day job" just cannot do.

Based on what I know now, my dream is

_____.

Don't get discouraged if you're not sure what your dream is yet. Remember that this is difficult for many people to identify. Sometimes you just have to experiment with something new (or a few things). Sometimes it's a matter of testing the waters by serving in a ministry area that seems interesting or attractive to you. Once you get involved, you might find something more specific within that ministry really speaking to your heart. Often we start with a general idea of what we want to do; and as we serve, our focus narrows and becomes much clearer.

It might make this process seem a little less nerve-racking if you keep in mind that your "dream"—where you want to make a difference in the world—may change over time. Whether that is due to life experiences, changing stages of life, or simply new interests/issues that spark your passion, your areas of focus DO sometimes shift. That's just the way it works. A corporate CEO who served primarily with mission projects on the weekends due to time constraints while he was working full time may find he has time to fulfill another of his dreams by attending choir practice and singing during worship once he retires.

It's important that you don't get stuck here. Stick with the journey. Keep hiking down the path. Trust God to reveal God's dream for you in God's own time.

Notes/Reflections on Dreams

test the waters

BE TOUCHED BY A DREAM

As you view the photos, check the ones that particularly touch or engage you. After all the pictures are viewed, your leader will read through the descriptions of the pictures so that you can look for patterns in your selections.

1. ☐ _____
2. ☐ _____
3. ☐ _____
4. ☐ _____
5. ☐ _____
6. ☐ _____
7. ☐ _____
8. ☐ _____
9. ☐ _____
10. ☐ _____
11. ☐ _____
12. ☐ _____
13. ☐ _____
14. ☐ _____
15. ☐ _____
16. ☐ _____
17. ☐ _____

18. ☐ _____
19. ☐ _____
20. ☐ _____
21. ☐ _____
22. ☐ _____
23. ☐ _____
24. ☐ _____
25. ☐ _____
26. ☐ _____
27. ☐ _____
28. ☐ _____
29. ☐ _____
30. ☐ _____
31. ☐ _____
32. ☐ _____
33. ☐ _____

Experiences

CHAPTER 6

Experiences

*We know that in all things God works for the good
of those who love him, who have been called
according to his purpose.*
—*Romans 8:28*

We all have a past. Good or bad—our experiences make us who we are today. Some people give themselves credit for the good things that happen to them and blame God for the bad. The reality is that we aren't responsible for all the good experiences, and God doesn't cause the bad experiences to happen to us—but God can use ALL of our experiences to fulfill God's purposes. Convicted in connection with the Watergate affair in the 1970s, Chuck Colson used his experiences in prison as a foundation for starting Prison Fellowship ministries across the country. Beverlee, a retired nurse, uses her experience as part of the Cardiac Attack Response Team at Church of the Resurrection. Whether our experiences are life experiences, ministry experiences, or simply circumstances, God can use them all for Kingdom benefit. Let's look at an example of each of these.

Mary was devastated when her husband of twelve years said he wanted to separate. They had two young daughters, and Mary wasn't sure where to turn. Though a woman of faith, Mary was depressed, hurt, and angry. A friend recommended that she call Alison, a woman in North Carolina whose husband had also asked for a separation.

When Mary finally worked up the courage to call and explained her situation, Alison immediately asked if she could pray for Mary right then, over the phone. Alison's voice seemed like that of an angel to Mary. The two women quickly became prayer partners even though a distance of one thousand miles separated them. Over the next two years as Mary's divorce finalized, Alison proved a tremendous support and encouragement for Mary.

Now Mary has the opportunity to offer that same support and encouragement to other women who are trying to make it through similar circumstances. God took Mary's life experience (although divorce is certainly not God's wish) and used it to allow her to help other people.

Many years ago, Yvonne was teaching Sunday school at a small church in Georgia (and was pretty happy doing that). When it was time to sign up for volunteer duties for the next year, a friend asked Yvonne to join the "visitation" team. The visitation team did just that—they visited all the first first-time visitors, welcomed them, and invited them to come to worship again.

Yvonne agreed, but became very sorry, very soon. A shy person, she found herself tongue-tied and sweaty-palmed when she walked up to a stranger's door. She was clumsy and stiff, and made others feel uncomfortable. She has said that she believes more people NEVER came back to her church after she visited than ever returned. It was a horrible experience for her. She began to think something was wrong with her, or that she was doing something wrong. Within a few months, Yvonne began to find reasons why she couldn't go to church on her team's week to do the visitation; and then, since she felt guilty for not showing up when she was supposed to, she quit going to church at all. But God wasn't quite finished with her yet. . . .

A few years later, Yvonne and her husband, Frank, moved to Kansas City. They visited the Church of the Resurrection. They loved it and decided to join, though Yvonne was determined not to sign up for anything. She did not want another ministry experience like the last one! When she heard about DISCIPLE Bible Study, she agreed to give it a try. Through that thirty-four weeks of study, Yvonne came to realize that we are all called to serve, but according to our spiritual gifts. It was like a lightning bolt striking her! She hadn't been doing anything wrong in her last ministry. She had been doing the wrong thing. She had not been using her spiritual gifts of teaching and leadership.

This experience gave Yvonne a real passion for helping others discover their spiritual gifts and find joy in using them to serve Christ. God used a bad ministry experience (though God doesn't plan for or desire for us to have bad ministry experiences) to bring Yvonne to the place God wants her to be, serving in the way God wants her to serve, and helping other people discover God's plan for them along the way.

Several years ago, Carol's husband, Jim, was transferred to Kansas City from Chicago. Carol had lived in Chicago all her life. She held the position of Director of Community Life at her home church, which meant she was responsible for the ministries that helped connect people to the life of the church. She determined her new "job" would be to help her family make the transition to their new home, job, and schools—she would take a sabbatical from church work until their lives were settled.

One Sunday after the move to Kansas City, as Carol sat in the sanctuary at the Church of the Resurrection, Pastor Adam Hamilton gave a sermon on the Parable of the Talents, relating it to our choice to either use or bury our God-given spiritual gifts. Carol felt the Holy Spirit urging her to put her own gifts to work in this new setting. Since her background was in equipping ministries, especially helping people discover and use their God-given gifts and talents, maybe there was a place for her to serve the church, and perhaps she needed to speak with Adam. However, she knew that he was always surrounded after the service and she wasn't really sure it was the right time to step back into a ministry. So she prayed, "Lord, if this is your will, help me connect with Adam." Amazingly, as Carol left the sanctuary, there stood Adam, momentarily alone.

She approached him, and Adam connected Carol with the Director of Discipleship at the church. She soon discovered that a member of the church staff had been praying for someone to help them develop a spiritual gifts ministry program. Once the connection was made, Carol helped form a team to start the gifts ministry. God used Carol's life circumstances to serve God's purposes.

When you think about it, all of our experiences—family experiences, work experiences, our relationships, our circumstances—are components of who we are and what we are prepared to do. Everything in life prepares us for our ministry, and it also allows us to be guides for others. In that sense, our experiences, good or bad, can draw us closer to God, and as we see God use those experiences for God's purposes, we develop a better understanding of God's will for our lives.

What experiences and circumstances in your life can God use for God's purposes?

How can you use them to help others?

Tapestry of My Life

How have your experiences shaped your life? Think about those milestones in your life—accomplishments, events or phases that have been defining or character-building in some way. Capture five of those experiences in just a few key words or phrases in the "bubbles" on the next page. Include the good and the bad, the inspiring and the challenging.

Spiritual Gifts and Experiences

NAME

Tapestry of My Life
Pick five important experiences or accomplishments in your life to briefly share with the group. Write key words about each in the bubbles.

PUTTING IT ALL TOGETHER

God is not unjust; he will not forget your work and the love
you have shown him as you have helped his people and
continue to help them. We want each of you to show this
same diligence to the very end, in order to make your hope
sure. We do not want you to become lazy, but to imitate
those who through faith and patience inherit what
has been promised.—Hebrews 6:10-12

Most of the time, when we hear the word *minister,* we think of a professionally trained person, serving in a paid staff position in our church. Rarely do we think of members of the church as "ministers." However, this is not an accurate reflection of the way the word was used in the New Testament.

The word *minister* comes from the translation of the Greek work *diakonia* which means "act of service." The word *deacon* traces its beginning to the word *diakonos*, which means "one who serves." Sometimes the word *deacon* is used in the New Testament to refer to special servants who meet certain qualifications specified in Acts 6:1-6 and 1 Timothy 3:8-13. But the word is also used in a more universal way to refer to all Christians in other passages. For example, in Ephesians 4:12, Paul speaks of God's people being equipped for "the work of ministry" (NRSV). The word used here is *diakonia*. Ministry is not an office, but an act of service. Every believer is a minister.

"But you are a chosen people, a royal priesthood, a holy nation, God's special possession, that you may declare the praises of him who called you out of darkness into his wonderful light."—1 Peter 2:9

The Dangers of Self-Reliance, Burnout, and Pride

We believe you are called to ministry. But as you serve, stay alert to three dangers that may threaten or tempt you. One is the danger of self-reliance and/or self-sufficiency. We sometimes get confused about the "ownership" of our gifts, talents, resources, and so forth, thinking they "belong" to us to use as we wish rather than treating them as gifts given by God. This can lead us to use what God has given us for our own benefit or might cause us to rely solely upon ourselves in ministry. The attitude we need to cultivate with regard to our gifts is one of stewardship, not ownership; and rather than keeping those gifts to ourselves, or relying on our own abilities and power, we need to place ourselves in a position of dependence on God. If you ever start thinking this way, stop and read Jesus' Parable of the Rich Fool in Luke 12:16-21. That parable and the realization that God has given you everything you have (and are) can help you get back on the right track of ministry again.

The second danger is that of burning out in your ministry. Burnout usually comes from one of three sources. One comes when we don't have enough instruction or guidance to feel that we are doing what we are supposed to be doing. Persons with a higher need for stability in their Individuality are especially susceptible to this kind of burnout. If this type of burnout seems to be happening to you, ask for more guidance, or shift to a different form of service quickly.

A second source of burnout comes when we don't support our ministry with personal time with God. We need to tend to our relationship with God even more carefully than a person might tend a garden.

Regular worship, daily prayer, Bible study, Christian fellowship, and Communion all nourish our spirits so that we can survive the times of dryness and conflict that inevitably will arise during Christian ministry.

A third source of burnout comes with boredom. Sometimes we have been at a task too long. We need to be refreshed, have a change of pace, learn or try something new. And it is okay to ask to be relieved from a ministry that you have been doing so you can take on a completely different project or task, or simply take a sabbatical—a sabbath (which, after all, is a good biblical term)—from the work you have been doing.

In other words, if you feel burnout coming on, ask for the help you need. Don't try to tough it out alone. God has placed you within the church among other Christians for a reason—so that you might support one another and bear one another's burdens!

Now, to the third danger: Please don't fall prey to the temptation of pride and become a so-called super-Christian. Because you have a certain gift or perceive you can do something better than someone else, don't ever think that you are better than they. God loves all of God's children the same. Your gifts are tools for you to use for God's glory, to lift up all God's people, and to build up God's kingdom.

Beyond these dangers, though, being in the service of God makes for a beautiful, wonderful life. It is the essence of true worship. For as we serve God, helping God's people and building God's kingdom, we truly give God the glory that God is due. It pleases God when we use the gifts God has given us to do what we were designed to do—which will not only serve Kingdom purposes, but will also bring us joy and satisfaction.

Find out what it is that God designed you to do—and then do it! We are all uniquely created, individually gifted children of God. God has a plan and purpose for your life. Trying to be something you are not is a no-win strategy. God has given you gifts according to God's will, and placed you in the body as God has determined. When you discover your S.T.R.I.D.E. and put it into action, you will find joy. You'll be realizing God's plan for your life!

The journey of faith is so much more fulfilling if we are in step with our own, unique God-given S.T.R.I.D.E.

May God bless you as you seek to know, love, and serve God.

Then Jesus came to them and said, "All authority in heaven and on earth has been given to me. Therefore go and make disciples of all nations, baptizing them in the name of the Father and of the Son and of the Holy Spirit, and teaching them to obey everything I have commanded you. And surely I am with you always, to the very end of the age."
—Matthew 28:18-20

"God has a Plan and Purpose for your Life."

S.T.R.I.D.E. MINISTRY PROFILE

I would like a one-on-one consultation: Yes_____ No _____

If yes, I prefer: Day _____ Evening _____

NAME _____ Day Phone: _____

E-mail: _____ Evening Phone_____

INSTRUCTOR: _____ Class Ending Date:_____

SPIRITUAL GIFTS: my three highest scoring spiritual gifts (in order) are:

1. _____

2. _____

3. _____

TALENTS: _____

_____

RESOURCES: _____

_____

INDIVIDUALITY: I believe my style is:

_____

DREAMS: I sense I have a passion for: _____

_____

EXPERIENCES: _____

_____

THREE POSSIBLE AREAS OF MINISTRY INVOLVEMENT

1.　_____

2.　_____

3.　_____

I AM ALREADY INVOLVED IN THE MINISTRY AREA OF

_____

Resources

Bugbee, Bruce. *What You Do Best in the Body of Christ.* Grand Rapids: Zondervan Publishing House, 1995.

Cartmill, Carol and Yvonne Gentile. *Leadership Essentials: Practical Tools for Leading in the Church.* Nashville: Abingdon Press, 2006.

_____. *Leadership from the Heart: Learning to Lead with Love and Skill.* Leader Kit. Nashville: Abingdon Press, 2004.

_____. *Leadership from the Heart: Learning to Lead with Love and Skill.* Participant Workbook. Nashville: Abingdon Press, 2004.

Chapman, Steven Curtis and Geoff Moore. *The Great Adventure.* Brentwood, TN: EMI Christian Music Publishing, 1992.

Cordeiro, Wayne. *Doing Church as a Team.* Honolulu: New Hope Resources, 1998.

Guiness, Os. *The Call: Finding and Fulfilling the Central Purpose of Your Life.* Nashville: Word Publishing, 1998.

Kent, Carol. *Secret Longings of the Heart.* Colorado Springs: NavPress, 1992.

Linn, Dennis, Sheila Linn and Matthew Linn. *Healing the Purpose of Your Heart.* Mahwah, NJ: Paulist Press, 1999.

Today's New International Version of the Bible. Copyright © 2005 by Biblica, Inc.™ Grand Rapids: Zondervan Publishing, 2005. www.zondervan.com